T·H·E G·R·E·A·T

CHEFS

OF VIRGINIA

by

The Virginia Chef's Association

Marcel Desaulniers, President

Compiled by Jonathan A. Zearfoss

Chef's portraits by Connie Desaulniers
Chapter illustrations by Victoria E. Burke

The Donning Company/Publishers
Norfolk/Virginia Beach

The Donning Company Publishers
5659 Virginia Beach Boulevard
Norfolk, Virginia 23502

Library of Congress Cataloging-in-Publication Data

The Great Chefs of Virginia Cookbook.

  Bibliography: p.
  Includes index.
  1. Cookery, International. 2. Cooks—Virginia—Biography.
I. Zearfoss, Jonathan A. II. Virginia Chefs Association
TX725.A1G7175   1987   641.5   87-5418
ISBN 0-89865-242-1 (pbk.)

Printed in the United States of America

CONTENTS

Special thanks to Nancy Rodrigues

Additional thanks to:
The Book Press, Williamsburg
Prince George Graphics, Williamsburg (Photography)
The Crawford Agency, Williamsburg
Mark Atkinson (Cover Photo)
Colonial Williamsburg (Photography)

FOREWORD

Dear Friends:

Culinary professionalism through education, apprenticeship, and fraternal association has been the goal of the Virginia Chefs since its inception in 1974. At that time, a handful of chefs from Richmond and Williamsburg organized to form a chapter of the American Culinary Federation. Today that chapter, the Virginia Chefs Association, is a diverse group of more than 100 chefs, bakers, cooks, and apprentices, all striving to improve the quality of their chosen profession.

In that light the creation of this book, *Cooking with the Virginia Chefs*, is another step toward enhancing the image of professional chefs in this country.

For too many years, chefs were not recognized as professionals. In 1986 the opposite holds true. Admissions to our top culinary schools is at an all time record high. A one-year wait for admittance to the Culinary Institute of America can be anticipated by hundreds of prospective culinarians.

The future has never been brighter for food service professionals. Consequently the future has also never been better for eating out in America. I believe that, after you have perused this book, you will agree that Virginia's chefs are bringing you some of the freshest, most creative, and best prepared food available in America today.

Enjoy and eat well,

Marcel A. Desaulniers CEC
President
The Virginia Chefs Association

The Dreamer

In Daydreams oft I contemplate
Great men I'd like to emulate,
And what my lifetime work would be
If such a choice were given me
An Armstrong landing on the moon?
A Rodgers with a lilting tune?
A Midas with his golden life?
A Ranier with a lovely wife?
A Horowitz with dazzling skill?
A Shakespeare with his magic quill?
A Brahms? Columbus? Rembrandt? Poe?
To one and all I'd answer "No!"
Let me instead some kitchen rule
As chef de cuisine proud, deft and cool
Ah, there's the talent! That's the life!
Keep your gold & take your wife!
Hang adventure! Music, pooh!
Poetry and drama, too!
As chef I'd fashion food supreme
With eggs and veal and wine and cream
I'd don a rakish snow-white toque,
And taking herbs and artichoke
Become composer, poet, king,
Explorer, artist, everything.

—Frank E. Potts
Gourmet, May 1975

=INTRODUCTION=

The interest in food and cooking which swept the country has been most influential in elevating the status of chefs in America.

Simultaneously, it has placed a heavy burden of responsibility on us to every day live up to the high expectations of an increasingly sophisticated and quality-demanding society.

In order to cope with this elevated status, chefs and cooks in America must constantly prepare and serve high quality food, which meets the needs of our society.

In this quest, nothing will serve us better than to turn to the basics and realize that the most exciting, sophisticated, and pleasing of dishes reflect an honest commitment to quality and simplicity.

"Nothing is harder than to prepare a simple, yet elegant, dish," quotes A. Escoffier, who taught us that simplicity and elegance are not in contrast to each other, but complement and enhance good cooking.

—Ferdinand E. Metz

President
Culinary Institute of America
Hyde Park, New York

Weights and Measures

Volume

1 gallon =4 quarts	=8 pints	=16 cups	=128 ounces
1 quart	=2 pints	=4 cups	= 32 ounces
1 cup	=8 ounces	=16 tablespoons	
½ cup	=4 ounces	= 8 tablespoons	
¼ cup	=2 ounces	= 4 tablespoons	
1 ounce	=2 tablespoons = 6 teaspoons		
1 tablespoon	=3 teaspoons		

Weight

1 pound =16 ounces
½ pound = 8 ounces
¼ pound = 4 ounces

—three measures of fresh chopped herbs equal 1 of dried
—one egg weighs about 2 ounces
—three cups of flour weigh about one pound
—one orange yields about 3 to 3½ ounces of juice
—one lemon yields about 1 to 1¼ ounces of juice

Terms and Abbreviations

Chop:	cut into small equal-size pieces
Cube:	from ½ inch to ¼ inch cube
Large Dice:	about ½ inch square
Dice or Medium Dice:	about ¼ inch square
Mince:	a very small dice
Fine Mince:	chopped as finely as possible by knife
Coarsely Ground:	a chunky powder, by mortar and pestle or by electric grinder
Ground:	a powder
Julienne:	sliced into fine strips
Poach:	to cook in simmering liquid (water or stock), perhaps enhanced by seasoning, herbs or wine
Pound:	abbreviated "lb."
Quart:	abbreviated "qt."
Roux:	a mixture of butter or other fat with flour for the purpose of the thickening, cooked to white, blond or brown depending on use
Tablespoon:	abbreviated "TBSP"
Teaspoon:	abbreviated "tsp"

SOUPS

> *...and the best cook*
> *cannot alter the first quality*
> *they must be good*
> *or the cook will be disappointed.*
>
> —Amelia Simmons
> *American Cookery*, 1796

Curried Apple and Onion

serves twelve

A. 2 TBSP cooking oil
  1 bunch celery (chopped)
  ½ med. onion (chopped)
  2 leeks (white part, chopped)
  ½ gal. chicken stock
  1 cup (2 sticks) butter
  ½ cup flour
  1 to 2 TBSP curry powder

B. 5 large onions (sliced)
  1 TBSP butter
  1 gal hot chicken stock
C. 3 Granny Smith apples
    (cored, quartered, and sliced)
  1 cup heavy cream
  Salt and pepper to taste

To prepare soup: In a heavy duty pot, heat the cooking oil. Sauté the celery, onions, and leeks for eight to ten minutes. In another pot bring chicken stock to a boil. In a separate pot make a roux by melting butter, then adding the flour and the curry powder. Cook thoroughly over medium heat, about ten minutes, stirring constantly. Add chicken stock to the roux. Stir until smooth. Add the vegetables and allow to simmer over medium heat for 45 minutes. Purée mixture in blender or food processor; keep hot.

In a heavy duty pot sauté the sliced onions in the one TBSP of butter until the onions are translucent. Add the hot chicken stock and allow to simmer until the liquid is reduced by one half of the original volume.

Combine the curried celery mixture and the onion mixture. Add the sliced apples and the heavy cream. Adjust the seasoning with salt and pepper. Serve piping hot.

—Marcel Desaulniers
The Trellis
Williamsburg

Potage Argenteuil

serves four

1 lb. asparagus, fresh, frozen
  or canned
1 TBSP butter
1 TBSP flour
1 qt. chicken consomme

1 qt. milk
1 tsp salt
½ tsp nutmeg
1 TBSP parsley, chopped
½ cup heavy cream

To prepare soup: Cut asparagus spears into ½ inch-pieces. Heat the butter in a saucepan, add the flour, and mix well. Warm the consommé and slowly add to the flour, stirring constantly. Add the milk. Stir in the salt and the nutmeg and mix well. Add the asparagus pieces. Cover the pan and simmer for 45 minutes.

Before serving, add the parsley and the cream.

Note: Potage Argenteuil can be prepared and frozen—but do not add the cream or the parsley. When soup is desired, defrost, reheat, add the cream and the parsley and serve.

—Paul Elbling
La Petite France
Richmond

Potage Laboureur

serves four

2 med. carrots
1 potato
1 onion
1 turnip
1 garlic clove
3 ounces ham
1 stalk celery (with leaves)
1 TBSP butter

4 TBSP split peas
2 qts. chicken consommé
3 ounces long noodles
2 tsp salt
½ tsp ground black pepper
½ tsp nutmeg
3 bay leaves
2 cloves

To prepare soup: Peel the carrots, potato, onion, and the turnip. Crush the garlic and dice the ham. Cut all of the vegetables into 1-inch pieces. Place the butter in a saucepan and add the vegetables. Sauté them for 5 minutes; then add the split peas, the chicken consommé, the noodles, and all seasonings, reserving the ham for garnish. Simmer the soup for 2½ hours. Let the soup cool a little and then purée it a bit in an electric blender. Mix the ham with the soup before serving.

An optional garnish would be croutons sautéed in butter. These can be sprinkled on top of the soup just before serving.

Note: The soup can be prepared, puréed, and frozen. When ready to serve, defrost the soup, warm it, add the ham as directed and serve.

—Paul Elbling
La Petite France
Richmond

Soup of Lamb, Barley, Red Peppers and Sage

serves eight

1 qt. lamb broth (see note)
4 strips bacon
2 med. onions
2 large garlic cloves
2 carrots
1 cup pearl barley
3 cups chopped (¼ in. cubed) lamb

4 TBSP pinenuts
2 small red bell peppers (or 1 large)
20 to 24 leaves fresh sage *or*
  2 TBSP chopped
Salt and freshly ground
  black pepper
Grated parmesan cheese as needed

To prepare soup: After making the broth, fry the bacon in a heavy duty pot until almost cooked. Add onion, garlic, and carrot. Sauté vegetables for two minutes and season lightly. Add the broth, the barley, and one quart water. Simmer the mixture for one half hour. Add the chopped lamb to the pot, bring the soup to a boil, and again reduce to a simmer. At this point toast the pinenuts at 300 degrees F. until golden brown (about 5 minutes). Split the red peppers in half, remove the seeds, and dice. Chop the sage. Crush the pepper and grate the parmesan. After barley has cooked for 1 hour (or is tender) add the sage and red peppers. Bring the soup to a boil, season, and garnish with the Parmesan cheese and the pinenuts.

Serve hot with crispy oven-hot Italian bread and lots of good butter.

Note: *To prepare lamb broth:* After enjoying a roasted leg of lamb, remove remaining meat and end cuts. This should be used for the chopped lamb. Break the bones and simmer in one gallon of water for several hours. Reduce liquid to one quart.

—Jonathan A. Zearfoss
The Trellis
Williamsburg

Cream of Squash and Leek

serves six

6 leeks
4 TBSP butter
2 lbs. squash
4 cups chicken stock

1 cup heavy cream
Salt and pepper to taste
1 ounce brandy (optional)

To prepare Soup: Wash and mince the white part of the leeks. In a large saucepan sauté the leeks in the butter until they are soft. Meanwhile, slice or dice the squash into 1-inch pieces. Add the squash to the saucepan and stir to warm. Add the chicken stock and bring to a boil. Simmer for 20 minutes. Stir in the heavy cream. Season with salt and pepper. If desired, add the brandy, strain and serve hot.

—Richard J. Nelson
Richmond

Spiced Meatball and Bean Soup

serves ten

1 lb. (2¼ cups) dry garbanzo beans
8 cups beef broth
4 cups water
½ cup onion (med. diced)
¼ cup onion (finely chopped)
½ cup green pepper (chopped)
2 TBSP parsley (snipped)
1¼ tsp salt

¼ tsp ground coriander
¼ tsp pepper
2 eggs (beaten)
1 TBSP milk
¾ cup soft bread crumbs
Dash ground cinnamon
Dash ground nutmeg
1 lb. ground beef

To prepare soup: In a dutch oven, mix the beans, four cups of the broth, and four cups of water. Bring to a boil and then simmer for two minutes. Remove from heat and let stand, covered, for one hour. Return to heat. Stir in the remaining broth, the medium diced onion, the green pepper, one TBSP parsley, ¼ tsp salt, the coriander and ⅛ tsp pepper. Simmer, covered, for 1¾ hours. Meanwhile make the meatballs.

To prepare meatballs: Combine eggs and milk; add crumbs, the minced onion, the remaining parsley, one tsp salt, ⅛ tsp pepper, the cinnamon, and the nutmeg. Add the ground beef; mix well. Shape this mixture into about forty meatballs using approximately one TBSP for each. Add the meatballs to the soup, cover, and simmer for 15 minutes. Serve.

—Art Cook
Westwood Racquet Club
Richmond

Ragout Español

serves four to six

3 TBSP butter or margarine
3 med. onions
2 stalks celery
1 med. carrot
2 tomatoes
1 TBSP garlic (chopped)
1 lb. beef

3 TBSP tomato paste
12 cups chicken stock
1 potato
½ tsp oregano
1 hot pepper (chopped)
Salt and pepper to taste
1 TBSP parsley (chopped)

To prepare soup: Chop the onions, the carrots, and the celery. Cube the tomatoes, the beef, and the potato.

In a heavy duty saucepan, melt the butter or margarine. Add the onion, celery, carrot, tomato, garlic, and the meat and sauté five minutes. Add the stock and the tomato paste. Add the potato and cook on medium heat for 25 minutes. Add the oregano and the hot pepper. Season with salt and pepper. Turn to low heat and cook soup for 25 minutes.

Before serving, sprinkle with parsley.

—Gideon Hirteinstein
Guest Services, Inc.
Washington, D.C.

The Trellis Cheese Soup

serves six

½ cup (1 stick) butter
½ cup flour
2 TBSP vegetable oil
1 large onion (sliced)
1 carrot (sliced)

2 stalks celery (sliced)
3 qts. hot chicken stock
¾ lb. Oregon Cheddar cheese
  (shredded)
Salt and pepper to taste

To prepare soup: In a heavy duty pot melt the butter. Add the flour and make a roux, cooking thoroughly, about 10 minutes. In a separate heavy duty pot, heat the oil; then sauté the vegetables for 5 minutes. Gradually add hot chicken stock to the cooked roux, stirring constantly until the mixture is smooth. Allow to simmer 10 minutes. Add the sautéed vegetables to the soup and allow to simmer until the vegetables are cooked. Remove the soup from the heat and gradually stir in the shredded cheese. Continue to stir until all the cheese has been added and

the soup is smooth. Adjust the seasoning with salt and pepper. Place the soup in a stainless steel container and hold in a hot water bath until service.

Note: At the Trellis we use an Oregon Cheddar called Tillamook. It is a bright yellow and firm cheese. This is the secret to this wonderful soup.

—Marcel Desaulniers
The Trellis
Williamsburg

Rabbit and White Bean Soup

serves eight

2 lb. navy beans
1½ qt. plus 1 TBSP water
1 TBSP vegetable oil
4 stalks celery (diced)
4 small leeks (white part only, diced)
2 med. onions (diced)

2 med. carrots (diced)
2 qt. chicken stock
2 TBSP butter
1 TBSP shallots (minced)
1 whole rabbit (boned and julienned)
2 TBSP fresh herbs (chopped)

To prepare the soup: In a large bowl, soak the white beans overnight in 1½ quarts of water. In a medium heavy pot, cook the beans for 30 to 35 minutes, until soft. While the beans are cooking, heat the oil and the one TBSP of water in a large pot. Sauté the celery, the leeks, the onion, and the carrots. Cook the vegetables thoroughly, about 10 minutes. Add the chicken stock to the vegetables. Drain the water from the cooked beans and add them to the pot with the stock. Cook the soup for 30 minutes. Pureé half of the mixture in a blender or food processor. Return the pureé to the soup. Bring the soup to a boil. If the soup is to be served immediately, reduce heat to low. The soup is best, however, if cooled and then reheated. Remove from the heat. In a medium sauté pan, melt the butter. Add the shallots and sauté briefly. Add the rabbit and the herbs and season lightly with salt and pepper. Cook the rabbit for about 5 minutes. Add the rabbit to the soup and cool.

For service: Bring the soup slowly to a boil, stirring occasionally. Season to taste and serve the soup immediately, piping hot.

—Jeff Duncan
The Trellis
Williamsburg

Soup of Squab and Wild Rice with Fresh Rosemary

serves four

2 fresh squab
1 med. carrot
1 stalk celery
1 onion
1 garlic clove
3 qt. water
½ cup wild rice

7 TBSP butter
½ cup flour
2 TBSP fresh rosemary (chopped)
4 sprigs rosemary
½ cup heavy cream
2 TBSP brandy or cognac

To prepare soup: Remove the skin of the birds and discard. Remove the breast and leg meat, reserve. Smash the bones with a cleaver; season liberally with salt and pepper. Cut the vegetables into pieces, trim, but do not bother to peel. Roast the carcasses, together with the carrot, celery, onion, and garlic at 500 degrees F. oven until well browned. After removing from the oven, put the bones and the vegetables in a heavy duty pot on the stove and cover with the water. Simmer for 1½ hours. Strain well.

In the strained broth, cook the wild rice, covered, at a simmer for one hour or until the rice just begins to bloom. Strain broth, reserve the rice, and return one quart of the broth to the stove (add water if necessary).

Heat two sauté pans, melting 2 TBSP of butter in one and 5 TBSP in the other. With a wire whisk stir the flour into the 5 TBSP butter and cook well (about 5 minutes or until the roux comes clean from the pan).

In the other pan sauté the squab; 1½ minutes on each side for breast meat and two minutes for the leg meat. Combine the roux with the now boiling stock, whipping vigorously until smooth. Return to a boil. Add chopped leg meat and chopped rosemary. Reduce to a simmer; add the wild rice. Stir in the cream and the brandy. Season with salt and pepper. Portion, and garnish each bowl with a sprig of rosemary and sliced breast meat.

Note: This soup can be made with any game bird (or chicken) compensating for size differences, of course.

—Jonathan A. Zearfoss
The Trellis
Williamsburg

Soup of Lobster, Goat Cheese and Fresh Salsa

serves four

Salsa:
1 ripe tomato
2 tomatilloes
1 large *or* 2 small garlic cloves
1 jalapeño pepper
⅛ tsp coriander
½ tsp fresh ground black pepper
2 TBSP balsamic *or* other
    sweet vinegar
2 green onions *or* scallions

2 1½-lb. lobsters
½ gal. water
2 cubes chicken bouillon
1 stalk celery
2 med. onions
½ cup butter
½ cup flour
½ lb. Monterey Jack cheese
8 ounces (one log) goat cheese

To prepare salsa: In boiling water submerge tomatoes for about thirty seconds (until skin begins to come loose); remove and plunge immediately into ice water. Remove skin, split in half horizontally, and remove seeds. Chop the tomatoes and the tomatilloes. Mince the garlic. On an electric burner on high or over a gas flame, char the skin on the jalapeño. Under cold running water remove the charred skin and, if desired, the seeds (the seeds will make the salsa spicier). Mince the jalapeño and thinly slice the scallion. Combine all ingredients and refrigerate.

To prepare soup: In the same boiling salted water as used in preparing the salsa, cook the lobsters for eight minutes. Cool. Remove the tail and the claws. Split the tail and remove the meat. Crack the claws and remove this meat. Cut the lobster meat into ½-inch cubes and refrigerate. Run the carcass under cool water to remove the roe and return all parts of the shell and carcass to one half gallon of the water. Add the bouillon cubes. Simmer for 1 hour; then bring to a boil and reduce liquid to one quart. While broth is simmering, grate the Monterey Jack and dice the onions and celery. Strain broth well. In a heavy duty saucepot, melt 2 TBSP butter. Sauté onions and celery 2 minutes and season lightly. Add the quart of broth to the vegetables and bring to a boil. In a sauté pan, melt 5 TBSP butter. Stir in flour and cook until the roux is smooth and comes clean from the pan (about 2 minutes). Combine the roux and the broth, whipping vigorously with a wire whisk until smooth and bring to a boil. Remove from heat and whisk in the grated Monterey Jack. Strain. Return to heat. *Do not boil!* In a sauté pan melt the remaining TBSP of butter. Break the goat cheese into ½-inch pieces. Distribute amongst bowls. Sauté lobster in the melted butter. Portion hot lobster. Pour hot soup into bowls over cheese and lobster. Garnish with a large dollop of chilled salsa.

—Jonathan A. Zearfoss
The Trellis, Williamsburg

Mobile Oyster Soup

serves eight

1 qt. oysters with juice
1 qt. half and half
2 TBSP butter
2 TBSP fresh parsley (minced)

2 TBSP spinach (minced)
⅛ tsp ground nutmeg
1 tsp onion (finely minced)
Salt and pepper to taste

To prepare soup: Strain oyster liquid into a saucepan and heat but do not boil. Heat the half and half and stir into the hot oyster broth. Add the butter, the parsley, the spinach, the nutmeg, and the onion. Add salt and pepper to taste. Add the oysters and as soon as they puff and crinkle at the edges, serve.

—Richard Perry, apprentice
The Trellis
Williamsburg

Seafood Chowder

serves four

3 lbs. fresh haddock
4 med. potatoes (diced)
3 med. onions (chopped)
12 fresh shucked clams
¼ lb. salt pork (diced)

8 saltine crackers
1 pint light cream
Salt and pepper to taste
1 TBSP butter

To prepare chowder: Cook the haddock in boiling, salted water, covered, until just done. Remove fish from water. Add the diced potatoes and the onions. In another pan, fry the salt pork until crisp. When the potatoes are soft, add the clams and the pork. Remove the skin and bones from the fish and add the haddock to the chowder. Split the crackers and soak them in one cup of the cream. Heat this mixture and when cream is hot add the mixture to the chowder. Season to taste with salt and pepper. Before serving add the butter and the remaining cream.

—Ted Kristensen
The Williamsburg Lodge
Williamsburg

11

Fish Chowder

serves six

1 lb. fish fillets (fresh *or* frozen)
2 cups potatoes (cubed)
2 tsp salt
⅛ tsp pepper

3 slices bacon
½ cup onion (med. diced)
2 cups milk
3 TBSP flour

To prepare soup: Cut the fish into two-inch pieces. Cook the potatoes in two cups of water, for 5 minutes. Add the fish, the salt, and the pepper. Simmer, covered, for 10 to 12 minutes. Cook the bacon until crisp. Drain and crumble; reserve the drippings. Sauté the onions in the bacon fat. Add the bacon and the onions to the fish mixture. Combine the milk and the flour, add to the chowder, stirring constantly. Cook until thickened. Serve.

—Art Cook
Westwood Racquet Club
Richmond

Seafood Gumbo

serves eight

2 med. onions
1 cup (2 to 3 stalks) celery
½ cup (1 small) green pepper
2 TBSP butter
¼ TBSP whole thyme
1 bay leaf
1½ tsp gumbo file
¾ tsp white pepper
1 tsp salt

4¾ cups seafood stock
1¼ cups crushed tomatoes
  (with juice)
¼ cup white rice
¼ lb. crabmeat
¼ lb. salmon *or* other firm fish
¼ lb. fresh *or* canned lobster
¼ lb. pearl shrimp
½ cup okra, frozen sliced

To prepare gumbo: Dice onions, celery, and green pepper. Sauté medium diced vegetables in butter until just tender. Add the thyme, the bay leaf, the gumbo file, the pepper, and the salt. Mix well. Add the stock, the tomatoes, and the rice. Simmer mixture for 30 minutes. Meanwhile, pick the crabmeat to remove cartilage. Cut the fish into ½-by-1-inch strips. Add the seafood and the okra. Simmer the gumbo 30 minutes longer. Serve hot.

—Mark Kimmel
The Tobacco Company
Richmond

Chef Willie Gumbo

serves eight to ten

1 med. onion (finely diced)
4 TBSP butter
½ cup rice
1⅓ cups chicken stock
1 tsp cayenne pepper
1½ lbs. fresh sausage *or*
   1 lb. smoked sausage
1½ cups vegetable oil
2 cups flour
5 med. onions (sliced)
8 ribs celery (sliced)

2 red peppers (seeded, sliced)
2 green peppers (seeded, sliced)
10 TBSP gumbo file
¾ gal. hot chicken stock
1½ lbs. fresh shrimp
   (peeled, deveined)
1 lb. tomatoes (peeled, seeded,
   and chopped)
1 small bunch scallions (sliced)
Salt and pepper to taste

To prepare the rice: Preheat the oven to 350 degrees F. In an ovenproof saucepot, sauté the finely diced onion in two TBSP of the butter. Add the rice and stir to coat the grains. Add the 1⅓ cup of chicken stock and the cayenne. Season the rice to taste with salt and pepper. Bring the stock to a boil, cover the saucepan and place in the oven for 15 to 20 minutes. Taste for doneness. Remove the rice and set aside.

To prepare the gumbo: Cut the sausage into ½ inch chunks, and cook over medium heat until done. Drain the sausage and set aside. In a thick pot heat the oil on high until very hot. Carefully whip in the flour and cook, stirring constantly until the roux is dark brown. In a separate pot, sauté the onions, the celery, and the peppers in two TBSP of butter with the gumbo file. Add the hot chicken stock to the vegetables and bring to a boil. Carefully whip in the hot roux and simmer the gumbo for 10 minutes. Add the shrimp and stir. Add the cooked sausage, the tomatoes, the cooked rice and the scallions. Season the gumbo to taste with salt and pepper. Serve hot.

—Philip Delaplane
The Trellis
Williamsburg

What one relishes, nourishes.

—Benjamin Franklin

Chilled English Stilton Soup

serves six

½ cup (1 stick) butter
½ cup flour
1 TBSP vegetable oil
4 stalks celery (large dice)
2 med. onions (large dice)
2 leeks (large dice)
½ gallon hot chicken stock

½ lb. Monterey Jack cheese (grated)
3 cups half and half
½ lb. Stilton cheese
    (broken into small chunks)
Salt and pepper to taste
6 pears (cored and diced)

To prepare soup: In a heavy duty pot melt the butter. Add the flour to make a roux, cooking thoroughly, about 10 minutes. In a separate heavy duty pot, heat the oil, then sauté the vegetables for 5 minutes. Add the hot chicken stock to the vegetables and bring to a boil. Stir the boiling stock into the cooked roux, continue to stir until all of the stock has been added and the mixture is smooth. Allow to simmer for 15 minutes. Remove the pot from the heat and gradually stir in the Monterey Jack until smooth. Strain the soup through a china cap. Cool the soup in an ice bath. When the soup is luke warm, add the half and half cream. When thoroughly cool, add the diced Stilton. Adjust the seasoning with salt and pepper. Before serving add the diced fresh pears.

Note: Rather than serve crackers as an accompaniment to the soup, consider a small round of flaky puff pastry with a touch of pear preserves.

—Marcel Desaulniers
The Trellis
Williamsburg

Chilled Gazpacho

serves twelve

6 large cucumbers
    (peeled, seeded, minced)
4 TBSP salt
4 large tomatoes
4 ounces pimento (chopped)
6 green onions (minced)
2 ounces vinegar
2 ounces olive oil

1 garlic clove (minced)
1 tsp sugar
Pinch cumin
1 qt. beef consomme (chilled)
1 qt. water
Salt and pepper to taste
1 TBSP chives
12 slices cucumber

To prepare soup: Mix the first five ingredients and set aside for one hour. Then add remaining ingredients and allow to set for 8 hours before

14

serving. Finish with chopped chives and top each bowl with a slice of cucumber.

—Ted Kristensen
The Williamsburg Lodge
Williamsburg

Chilled Cherry Soup

serves twelve

2 11-ounce cans pitted black
   cherries in syrup
1 qt. unsweetened grape juice
½ cup burgundy wine
Pinch cinnamon

Pinch nutmeg
2 TBSP arrowroot
2 TBSP Kirschwasser
12 sprigs fresh mint

To prepare soup: Reserving one half cup of grape juice, combine the first five ingredients in a saucepan and bring to a boil. Combine arrowroot with the reserved grape juice and whip this mixture into the boiling soup. As soon as the soup begins to thicken, remove from heat and chill. Before serving add the Kirschwasser. Garnish each bowl with a mint sprig.

—Ted Kristensen
The Williamsburg Lodge
Williamsburg

> *...Such as we found in the fort, had we stayed but four days, had doubtless been the most part of them starved, for their best relief was only mushrooms and some herbs which, sod together, made but a thin and unsavory broth and swelled them much.*
>
> *—"A True Reportory of the Wreck and Redemption of Sir Thomas Gates, Knight, upon and from the Islands of the Bermudas: His Coming to Virginia and the Estate of that Colony Then and After, under the Government of the Lord La Warr, July 15, 1610.*
>
> *written by William Strachey, Esquire"*

Chilled Strawberry Soup

serves ten

2 pints fresh strawberries
  (sliced)
Pinch allspice
1 TBSP lemon juice

½ cup sugar
1 qt. water
2 TBSP tapioca
2 cups buttermilk

To prepare soup: In a heavy duty saucepan, combine all ingredients except tapioca and buttermilk. Bring to a boil. Add the tapioca and stir to thicken. Chill and add buttermilk. Serve.

—Ted Kristensen
The Williamsburg Lodge
Williamsburg

Watercress and Sorrel Vichyssoise

serves eight

4 TBSP unsalted butter
1 cup leeks (diced)
½ cup onion (chopped)
½ cup watercress
½ cup sorrel
3 cups potatoes (thinly sliced)

1 cup bay leaf
4 cups chicken stock
1 cup water
2 cups milk
Salt and white pepper to taste
2 cups heavy cream

To prepare the chilled soup: Melt the butter in a heavy saucepan. Add the leeks, the onion, the watercress and the sorrel. Sauté over medium heat until the vegetables are tender. Do not allow to brown. Add the potatoes, the bay leaf, the chicken stock, and the water. Bring to a boil, reduce the heat, and simmer, uncovered, for 20 minutes or until the potatoes are soft. Discard the bay leaf. Purée the soup in a blender or food processor. Return the soup to the heat and add the milk. Simmer for 10 minutes. Strain the soup thoroughly. Taste again for seasoning after the soup has cooled. Stir in the cream just before serving. Garnish with sorrel and watercress.

—Hans Schadler
The Williamsburg Inn
Williamsburg

APPÉTIZERS

HOT APPETIZERS

> *The grand arcanum of management*
> *Lies in three simple rules:*
>
> —*"Let Everything to be done at*
> *the proper time,*
> *Keep everything in its proper place,*
> *And put everything to its proper use."*
>
> —Mary Randolph

Chicken Livers in Red Wine Wrapped in Bacon

serves twenty-five

1½ lbs. chicken livers
Salt and pepper to taste
3 TBSP butter

24 strips bacon
½ to 1 cup red wine

To prepare the hors-d'oeuvre: Clean the livers, remove the membrane, cut to portion size (½ liver) and season with salt and pepper. Heat a skillet and melt the butter. Add the livers, sauté a few minutes, and then add the wine. Sauté 2 more minutes; then remove from heat and cool. Wrap each portion in a half strip of bacon. Fasten with a toothpick. Place the hors-d'oeuvres on a broiler pan about two to three inches from the heating unit. Broil on each side until the bacon is done.

Serve the hors-d'oeuvres in a chafing dish.

—Ted Kristensen
The Williamsburg Lodge
Williamsburg

Seafood Quiche

serves eight

Crust
1 10-inch pie shell
1 egg
⅓ cup milk

Filling
4 TBSP butter
½ lb. bay scallops (if using
    sea scallops, cut into
    ½-inch pieces)
¾ lb. pearl shrimp
1¼ lbs. lump crabmeat
1 green onion (chopped)

5 eggs
½ cup half and half
¼ tsp. black pepper
¼ tsp. seafood seasoning
¾ lb. provolone cheese (grated)
¼ tsp salt
Pinch thyme
1 TBSP fresh parsley (chopped)

To make the quiche: Preheat the oven to 225 degrees F. Prepare an egg wash of egg and milk by stirring until well mixed. Brush the egg wash on the pie shell until well coated. Lightly prick the bottom of the shell. Bake the shell for 12 to 15 minutes or until the shell is lightly browned. Set the shell aside. In a large skillet melt the butter. Sauté the scallops, the shrimp, the crabmeat and the onion until the scallops are just opaque. Set the seafood mixture aside. Stir all remaining ingredients together until well mixed. Combine these with the seafood. Pour all into the pie shell. Bake at 225 degrees F. for approximately 1 hour and 10 minutes, or until set (slightly firm to the touch).

—Mark Kimmel
The Tobacco Company
Richmond

Sauerkraut Balls

serves six

3 TBSP butter
1 small onion (minced)
½ tsp chopped garlic
2 cups corned beef (ground)
1 cup flour, divided
½ cup beef stock

1 TBSP chopped parsley
2 cups sauerkraut (chopped)
2 eggs
1 TBSP water
2 cups stale bread crumbs

To prepare the appetizer: In a sauté pan, melt the butter. Sauté the onion and the garlic. To the pan, add the corned beef and seven TBSP of the flour. Cook, stirring, until smooth. Add the beef stock, the parsley, and the sauerkraut. Continue to cook until the mixture is smooth. Spread the sauerkraut mixture on a platter and cool. When cool, form the mixture into 1-inch balls and bread them one by one; first roll them in four then dip them in a combined egg and water mixture and finally roll them in the bread crumbs. Deep-fry the balls at 375 degrees F. until golden.

Serve the appetizer hot with mustard.

—Mitford Sims III
The Tobacco Company
Richmond

Cheese Cookies

serves six

1 lb. sharp Cheddar cheese (grated)
2 cups (4 sticks) butter
4 cups flour, sifted

tabasco to taste
1 lb. pecan halves

To prepare cookies: Preheat oven to 450 degrees F. Cream the grated cheese and the butter together. Add the flour and the tabasco. *Do not overmix!* Refrigerate the dough for 1 hour. Roll out and cut the dough into 1¼-inch cookies. Place the cookies on an ungreased cookie sheet and bake, each with a pecan on top, for 7 to 8 minutes or until lightly golden.

—Mitford Sims III
The Tobacco Company
Richmond

Asparagus and Smoked Salmon on Lemon Pasta

serves four

Pasta
2 cups flour
1 TBSP lemon zest (minced)
2 eggs plus 1 egg yolk
2 TBSP fresh lemon juice
1 TBSP olive oil

½ tsp salt
16 spears asparagus (peeled)
8 ounces smoked salmon
   (¼-inch cubes)
2 TBSP butter, divided
Parmesan cheese (optional)

To make the pasta: Combine flour, salt, and lemon zest and make a small mound with these on a wide counter. In a bowl beat the eggs and the yolk, the lemon juice and the olive oil. Make a well in the center of the flour mixture. Incorporate the flour from the outside in with a fork until the mixture forms a ball. Work the ball with your hands until it is smooth and elastic. Cover and set the dough aside for at least 1 hour before cutting. Roll the pasta through a pasta machine until desired thickness is achieved. Cut the pasta into the desired shape. Fettuccine (wide flat noodle) is recommended.

To prepare the appetizer: Trim root end of the peeled asparagus spears and cut into two-inch pieces. Drop the pieces into boiling salted water and cook for about 3 minutes, or until tender. Remove and place them immediately in ice water. (This step can be done one day in advance). Melt one TBSP of the butter in a sauté pan. Sauté the asparagus and the salmon until just hot; season to taste. Meanwhile, cook the pasta in boiling salted water until al dente (about 30 seconds). Toss remaining butter with the freshly cooked pasta.

Serve immediately with grated Parmesan (if desired).

—Michael Gyetvan
The Trellis
Williamsburg

Braised Seafood with Tomatoes and Basil Noodles

serves six

Pasta
2⅓ cups hi-gluten flour, divided
2 eggs
1 egg yolk
¼ cup fresh basil (chopped)
2 TBSP water
1 tsp olive oil
½ tsp salt
Cornmeal as needed

2 TBSP butter
2 large shallots (chopped)
3 ripe tomatoes (peeled,
  seeded and chopped)
Salt and fresh ground black pepper
2 8-ounce bottles clam juice
1 cup water (*or* use 3 cups water
  and 2 chicken bouillon cubes)
¼ cup dry white wine

Pinch saffron
1½ dozen (12 to 15 count) shrimp
  (peeled and deveined)
1½ dozen littleneck clams
  (in shells)
1½ dozen mussels (in shells)
2 TBSP cornmeal
1½ dozen Va. oysters (shucked)

To make the pasta: In a mixing bowl, put two cups of flour forming a well in the center. Combine the next six ingredients and fill the well with these. Using a fork, move the flour from the outside towards the well, until all is mixed. Flour a marble cutting board or other cool surface. Knead the dough on the board, occasionally flouring the board, until the dough will accept no more flour. You cannot overknead this dough by hand. Let dough rest, well-wrapped, for at least 1 hour. Roll the dough into sheets on a pasta machine to the desired thickness, about 1/16 inch. Cut the pasta sheets with a rolling ravioli cutter or a knife into noodles about ½ inch wide. Dust the noodles lightly with cornmeal and cover.

To prepare the appetizer: In a large saucepot or skillet, melt the butter. Sauté the shallots briefly; then add the tomatoes and season lightly with salt and pepper. Add the clam juice, the water, the white wine and the saffron. Bring the mixture to a good simmer. Add the shrimp. After 30 seconds, add the clams, which have been thoroughly washed in cold water. After 1 minute add the mussels, which have been scrubbed and then cleansed in cold water with cornmeal. As soon as the mussels begin to open, add the oysters. Toss the pasta to remove the cornmeal and, being careful to separate the noodles, add them to the pot. Adjust the seasoning. Cook until pasta is just al dente, about 30 to 45 seconds.

Serve immediately with a crisp white wine and grated Parmesan cheese if desired.

—Jonathan A. Zearfoss
The Trellis
Williamsburg

Meat and Cheese Bread

serves four

1¼ cups lukewarm milk
1 TBSP salt
6 TBSP olive oil
1 TBSP yeast
3½ to 4 cups hi-gluten

6 TBSP Parmesan cheese
  (grated), divided
¼ cup pepperoni (small dice)
¼ cup salami (small dice)
½ TBSP butter
flour

To prepare the bread: Prepare oven to 400 degrees F. In a small saucepan, scald the milk together with the salt and four TBSP of the oil. Transfer to a mixing bowl and cool to lukewarm. Dissolve the yeast in the milk mixture. Slowly stir in the flour until dough is stiff enough to knead. Turn the dough out onto a floured surface and knead until smooth. Place the dough in a large oiled bowl. Cover and let rise until doubled in size. Punch a hole in the middle of the dough and fill with four TBSP of the cheese and the meat. Knead the dough for a few minutes working the cheese and meat throughout the dough. Place dough into a buttered 9-by-5-inch loaf pan. Combine 2 TBSP of oil with 2 TBSP of the Parmesan and brush the dough with this topping. Let rise until doubled in size. Bake for 35 to 40 minutes.

—Joe Wilson, apprentice
The Trellis
Williamsburg

Spicy Sautéed Mussels in Dry White Wine

serves four

6 TBSP butter
1 med. onion (chopped)
2 small green peppers (chopped)
1 chile pepper (chopped)
1 med. tomato (small cubes)
2 tsp garlic (fresh chopped)
½ tsp oregano

½ tsp Hungarian paprika
1 cup dry white wine
2 dozen large mussels (shucked)
Salt and pepper to taste
4 round garlic toasts
2 tsp chopped parsley
1 lemon (four wedges)

To prepare the appetizer: In a hot sauté pan, melt the butter. Add the onion, the peppers, the chile pepper and the tomato and sauté for 2 to 3 minutes. Add the garlic, the oregano, the paprika and the wine. Mix all well and cook for 2 to 3 more minutes. Add the mussels. Cook for 5 minutes on medium heat. Divide the mixture equally between four casserole dishes. Serve with a toast round and the parsley for garnish and the lemon wedge on the side, immediately.

—Gideon Hirteinstein
Guest Services, Inc.
Washington, D.C.

Zwiebelkuchen
(Swiss Onion Pie)

serves six

1 lb. pie dough
1 lb. onions
3 TBSP butter
2 TBSP bacon (diced)
1 TBSP flour

2 eggs
1½ cups half and half
1 tsp salt
Pepper to taste

To prepare the pie: Preheat oven to 375 degrees F. Roll out and then spread the dough on a baking tin. In a skillet heat the butter and then fry the bacon. Add the onions and braise them on low heat, covered, until they have a glassy appearance. Prepare a batter with the flour, the eggs, the half and half, and the salt. Add the braised onions. Mix well and season with pepper. Spread the mixture evenly on the prepared dough. Bake until crust is golden, about 30 minutes.

—Otto Bernet
Chef Otto's Bakery
Richmond

Stuffed Deviled Clams

serves six

1 pint shucked clams *or 2*
    7½ cans minced clams
1 tsp ground mace

1 tsp ground nutmeg
2½ cups soft bread crumbs
4 TBSP butter (melted)

To prepare the appetizer: Preheat oven to 375 degrees F. Drain and coarsely chop the fresh clams (or drain the canned clams). Stir in the mace and the nutmeg. Spoon into six greased individual baking shells. Toss the bread crumbs with the melted butter. Sprinkle the buttered crumbs over the clams. Bake, uncovered, for 15 minutes.
    Serve the clams hot.

—Art Cook
The Westwood Racquet Club
Richmond

Baked Onions with Meat Stuffing

serves four

4 med. (2 lb.) onions
2 eggs (beaten)
2 cups beef, lamb, or pork
(cooked and finely chopped)
¼ cup chopped fresh red bell
pepper *or* canned pimento
2 TBSP parsley (snipped)

¾ cup bread crumbs
1 tsp salt
½ tsp dried oregano
⅛ tsp pepper
½ fresh red bell pepper *or* canned
pimento (cut in strips)
½ cup boiling water

To prepare the appetizer: Peel the onions and cook them, covered, in a large amount of boiling water until nearly tender, about 20 minutes. Drain the onions and cool. Preheat oven to 350 degrees F. Remove the tops and the centers of the onions to form shells about ¼ inch thick. Chop the centers and reserve two TBSP (use the remaining onion elsewhere). Mix the eggs and the bread crumbs. Add the meat, the red pepper, the parsley, the salt, the oregano, the pepper and the reserved chopped onion. Mix well. Lightly sprinkle salt inside the onion shells and fill with the meat mixture. Place the stuffed onions in an 8-by-8-by-2-inch baking dish. Garnish the tops with the strips of red pepper. Pour the boiling water into the dish. Bake, covered, until the onions are tender and the stuffing is heated through, about 30 minutes.

—Art Cook
Westwood Racquet Club
Richmond

Panfried Black Turtle Bean Cakes with Tequila and Horseradish Sauce

serves four to six

Bean cakes
1 lb. black turtle beans
½ cup onion (finely diced)
4 tsp garlic (minced)
3 tsp basil leaves (chopped)
4 tsp salt
1 jalapeño pepper
(seeded and minced)
2 egg yolks

Sauce
8 ounces sour cream
3 TBSP chives (chopped)
1 TBSP tequila
1 TBSP fresh grated horseradish
Salt and pepper to taste

To prepare the bean cakes: Preheat oven to 350 degrees F. In eight cups of boiling salted water, cook the black turtle beans until al dente. Allow the beans to cool; then drain them of any excess liquid and crush them with a slotted spoon. Combine the beans with the next 6 ingredients. When all the ingredients are thoroughly combined, form the mixture into 3-ounce balls. Roll the balls in flour and then press them flat. Saute the bean cakes in a small amount of butter until browned on both sides. Finish heating the cakes for 4 to 6 minutes. Serve hot with two ounces of tequila and horseradish sauce.

To prepare the sauce: In a mixing bowl whip the sour cream with a wire whisk until smooth. Combine all ingredients. Put two ounces in a small ramekin.

Serve two hot bean cakes with a small ramekin of the chilled sauce. Garnish the plate with watercress and red grapes.

—Marcel Desaulniers
The Trellis
Williamsburg

Grilled Skewer of Snails and Chicken

serves six

36 snails	2 TBSP brandy
3 TBSP butter	Salt and pepper to taste
½ cup shallots (chopped)	¾ lb. lemon marinated chicken
2 TBSP garlic (minced)	breast strips
¼ cup dry white wine	1 large red pepper (cubes)

To prepare the snails: Sauté the snails in butter with the shallots, the garlic, the white wine, the brandy, and the salt and pepper. Cook for 10 to 15 minutes or until almost all the liquid is evaporated. Allow the snails to cool.

To prepare the skewers: Alternately skewer the snails (six per skewer), the chicken meat, and the red pepper cubes onto six bamboo skewers. Grill the skewers over a low charcoal fire; brush with butter while cooking.

As an appetizer serve the skewer on a bed of pasta or rice pilaf. As an hors-d'oeuvre serve on smaller skewers.

—Marcel Desaulniers
The Trellis
Williamsburg

> *Hunger is the best pickle.*
>
> —Benjamin Franklin

Mushrooms Nantua

serves eight

1 med. onion
1¼ lb. crabmeat
5 TBSP butter
2¾ cups Mornay sauce (see index)
¾ tsp white pepper
1 TBSP lemon juice

2 to 3 drops tabasco
¾ tsp salt
3 TBSP dry sherry
50 mushroom caps
¾ cup Hollandaise sauce (see index)

To prepare mushrooms: Chop the onion and the crabmeat, each very fine. Sauté the onion in butter until transparent. Add the crabmeat and simmer gently. In a separate pan, warm the Mornay sauce slowly. To the onions and crabmeat, add 1¼ cup of sauce, the pepper, the lemon juice, the tabasco, the salt and the sherry. Stir until well mixed. Remove from heat and allow to cool. Remove stems from mushrooms. Wash and dry caps. Using a pastry bag (large plain tip) or spoon, stuff caps with the crab mixture, approximately one TBSP per cap.

For service: In the bottom of a serving dish, spread the remaining Mornay sauce (1½ cups). Top the sauce with the stuffed mushrooms. Top the mushrooms with the Hollandaise sauce. Glaze the appetizers lightly under a broiler.

Serve immediately with lemon wedges.

—Mark Kimmel
The Tobacco Company
Richmond

27

Vegetables Mornay En-Croute

serves four

1 cup Mornay sauce (see index)
2 TBSP butter
1 carrot (diced)
4 cauliflower florets (cut very small)
1 stalk celery (sliced thin)

1 green pepper (julienne cut)
4 broccoli florets (cut very small)
½ red onion (julienne cut)
Salt and pepper to taste
1 4-by-16-inch sheet puff pastry

To prepare the appetizer: Preheat oven to 350 degrees F. Prepare the sauce, hold warm. In a sauté pan, melt the butter. Sauté the carrots, the cauliflower, and the celery briefly; then add the green pepper, the broccoli, and the onion. Add salt and pepper. Continue to sauté until all the vegetables are al dente. Add the Mornay sauce to the vegetables and simmer for 4 minutes. Remove from heat, hold warm. Thaw the puff pastry (if frozen) and cut into 4-inch squares. Place two to three TBSP of the mornay and vegetable mixture in the center of each square. Fold the pastry over and crimp the edges with a fork. Brush with an eggwash (one beaten egg and two TBSP water) if desired, and bake until golden, 30 to 40 minutes.

Serve immediately.

—Daniel Ayers
Richmond

Artichoke and Broccoli Mousseline

serves four

4 fresh artichokes
1 tsp lemon juice
4 broccoli florets (cooked)

Sauce
1 cup Hollandaise sauce (see index)
¼ cup heavy cream (whipped)

To prepare the sauce: Fold together the hollandaise and the cream.

To prepare the appetizer: Cook fresh artichokes in boiling, salted water with lemon juice for 10 to 12 minutes. Drain. Trim the outer leaves. Cut off the top. Cut in half and remove the choke. Place the cooked broccoli floret in the center. Top with sauce and serve.

—Richard J. Nelson
Richmond

Braised Wild Mushrooms,
Asparagus and Tomatoes

serves six to eight

1 lb. fresh wild mushrooms *or*
   ¼ lb. dry (rehydrated in 2 cups
   warm water)
¾ lb. asparagus
¾ lb. tomatoes
2 shallots

6 cups mild chicken stock (hot,
   if using dry mushrooms use
   rehydrating liquid for stock)
2 TBSP white wine
Salt and pepper to taste

To prepare the appetizer: Clean and slice the wild mushrooms. Lightly peel and trim the asparagus. Slice the asparagus on a bias into 1-inch pieces. Plunge the cored tomatoes into boiling, salted water for 30 seconds and then into ice water. Remove the skins, cut the tomatoes in half horizontally, remove the seeds, and chop them into ½-inch cubes. Peel and mince the shallots. In a large pan, place the shallots and the white wine. Cook for 2 minutes over medium high heat. Add the mushrooms, the asparagus, the tomatoes and one cup of the stock. Cook the mixture for 3 to 4 minutes. Add the remaining stock and bring to a light boil. Season with salt and pepper to taste and serve piping hot with crusty French bread.

Note: If fresh tarragon or thyme is available, add a bit of that to the braised mushrooms.

—Philip Delaplane
The Trellis
Williamsburg

Chesapeake Crab Puffs

serves six

1 small onion (fine dice)
1 stalk celery (fine dice)
1 to 2 TBSP butter
1 6-by-10-inch sheet puff pastry
1 TBSP Dijon-style mustard

1 lb. blue crab
   (picked to remove shell
Salt and pepper to taste
1 egg (beaten)
1 TBSP water

To prepare the puffs: Preheat oven to 350 degrees F. Sauté the onion and celery in butter until tender. Remove from heat. Roll out the pastry dough and, using a pastry brush, spread thinly with mustard. Mix the onion and celery with the crabmeat. Season to taste.

   Place the crabmeat mixture (about two TBSP) on a 3-inch square of

29

puff pastry. Pull the sides of the pastry up equally and twist the top to seal (if not sealed properly, they will open during baking). Beat the egg and the water together to make an egg wash and brush on the pastry. Bake about 10 minutes, until golden brown. The puffs may be served as is, or with numerous sauces (cocktail, mornay, cheese, etc.)

—David Jordan
The Virginia Museum
Richmond

. . .He stayed in Richmond several days, living sumptuously in the splendid hotel, eating from silver dishes in the grill, and roaming pleasantly through the wide streets of the romantic old town, to which he had come once as a Freshman at Thanksgiving, when the university's team had played Virginia there. He spent three days trying to seduce a waitress in an ice-cream and candy store: he lured her finally to a curtained booth in a chop-suey restaurant, only to have his efforts fail when the elaborate meal he had arranged for with the Chinaman aroused her distaste because it had onions in it.

—Thomas Wolfe
Look Homeward Angel, 1929

CHILLED APPETIZERS

> ...*she set on the bord...sodden venison, and rosted fish; in the like manner mellons raw, boyled roots and fruites of divers kinds. There drinke is commonly water boyled with Ginger, sometimes with Saxafras, and wholesome herbes, but whilest the grape lasteth they drink wine.*
>
> —Capt. John Smith
> *The General Historie of Virginia...*, 1584

Tuscan Tart al Berto

serves six

1 med. eggplant
2 med. summer squash
¼ cup olive oil, divided
Salt to taste
1 16-by-10-inch sheet puff pastry
1 cup tomato sauce (see note)
½ tsp fresh ground black pepper

3 ounces Parmesan cheese
1 TBSP fresh sweet basil
½ tsp fresh ground fennel seeds
½ cup pitted alphonso olives
½ lb. fennel sausage
10 ounces ricotta cheese
4 ounces fontina cheese

To prepare this hearty peasant appetizer: Preheat oven to 350 degrees F. Wash the eggplant and the squash. Slice both lengthwise ⅛-inch thick. In a hot skillet, briefly sear the slices in about one TBSP olive oil, adding more oil as necessary. Season with a pinch of salt and pat dry with a paper towel when cool. Place the puff pastry sheet in an oblong ten-inch glass dish. Arrange the eggplant slices in a shingle pattern on top of the pastry. Spread a thin coating of the tomato sauce on the eggplant. Sprinkle one third each of the pepper, the Parmesan, the herbs and the olives over the sauce. Next arrange thinly sliced sausage on top of the cheese and herbs. Spoon on pieces of ricotta the size of a shelled pecan. Place slices of squash on top and repeat the procedure. When tart is 1½ inches high, gently press down on the top layer of squash, forcing out air and compressing the layers. Sprinkle grated fontina on top and bake for 20 minutes. Cover with foil and bake 15 more minutes at 250 degrees F. Cool uncovered; then refrigerate the tart *overnight*.

Cut the tart into thin slices and serve chilled with dry white wine.

Note: If using a prepared sauce, be sure it is a thick recipe.

—Robert B. Ramsey
Richmond

Terrine de Saumon

serves six

1 lb. fresh salmon	**Panada**
2½ tsp salt	1 cup water
1 tsp ground white pepper	½ cup (1 stick) butter
¼ cup cognac	1 cup flour
½ cup ruby port	4 whole eggs
1 lb. fresh rockfish *or* bluefish	
½ tsp nutmeg	½ lb. sliced bacon (uncooked)
	¼ cup shelled pistachio nuts (whole)

To prepare the appetizer: Marinate the salmon in a dish within one tsp salt, ½ tsp pepper, the cognac, and the port for 1 hour, turning on both sides so the fish can best absorb the flavors. Grind the rockfish (or bluefish) and add to it one tsp salt, ½ tsp pepper, and the nutmeg. Set aside to mix later with the cooled panada. While the salmon is marinating, make the panada. Preheat oven to 350 degrees F.

To prepare the panada: Place the water and the butter in a pan and bring to a boil. Add the flour all at once, stirring briskly. Remove the pan from the fire and then add the eggs, one at a time. Beat well after each addition and set aside to cool.

To prepare the terrine: When the panada is completely cool, add the rockfish mixture.

Line a loaf pan with the uncooked bacon slices, overlapping them slightly. Fill the loaf pan alternately with layers of the panada mixture and of salmon. Sprinkle the pistachio nuts between the layers. Cover the pan with aluminum foil. Place the covered pan into a water bath. For the bath, use a larger, high baking dish, at least two inches higher. Add as much water as to safely fill.

Bake for 1½ hours. This technique will actually steam the salmon terrine. When finished baking, let the terrine cool, remove it from the pan and place it in the refrigerator to chill.

Serve this terrine also as a main course for four. The terrine is best accompanied by a Riesling, Chablis, or Sauvignon Blanc.

—Paul Elbling
La Petite France
Richmond

Williamsburg Inn Chilled Shrimp and Crab Gumbo

serves twelve

Bouquet garni
6 stems parsley (chopped)
1 garlic clove (minced)
½ tsp leaf thyme
½ tsp leaf marjoram
2 bay leaves

½ cup celery (fine chopped)
½ cup onion (fine chopped)
½ cup green pepper (fine chopped)
½ cup leeks (fine chopped)

1 lb. crabmeat (cooked)
1 lb. baby shrimp (cooked)
Pinch saffron
1 cup okra (chopped) (see note)
1 cup tomatoes (chopped)
1 tsp salt (or to taste)
½ tsp white pepper
½ tsp gumbo file powder (see note)
1 envelope unflavored gelatin
½ cup warm water
1 cup rice (cooked)

To prepare the gumbo: Prepare the bouquet garni by tying the herbs in a cheesecloth bag. Heat two quarts of water to boiling and add the bouquet garni, the celery, the onion, the green pepper, and the leeks. Cover the pot and simmer for 20 minutes. Pick over the crabmeat and remove any bits of shell or cartilage. Add the crabmeat, the shrimp and the saffron to the simmering vegetables. Allow the mixture to simmer slowly for 15 minutes. Add the okra. Add the tomatoes, the salt and the pepper. Remove ½ cup of the liquid from the pot, add to it the file powder, and beat together thoroughly. Stir the mixture into the pot. Be careful not to let the soup boil after the file powder is added or it will become stringy and unfit to serve. Soften the gelatin in warm water. Remove the pot from the heat and stir in the softened gelatin. Add the cooked rice and adjust the seasoning. Refrigerate the gumbo, overnight if possible, to bring out the flavor. Serve in cold cups.

Note: If canned okra is used the liquid should be added to the gumbo after the cooking process as it will enhance the flavor of the soup. If raw okra is used, blanch it in two cups of the stock before adding it to the gumbo. Return the liquid to the gumbo as well.

Note: If file powder is not available, the okra will be sufficient however, gumbo tastes better when both okra and file powder are used.

—Hans Schadler
The Williamsburg Inn
Williamsburg

Peach Halves Stuffed with Duck Livers

serves eight

4 med. fresh peaches	2 tsp garlic (minced)
5 tsp butter or margarine	½ tsp tarragon
1 lb. duck livers	Salt and black pepper to taste
1 med. onion (chopped)	8 leaves iceberg lettuce
3 tsp chopped parsley	1 red bell pepper
1 hard-cooked egg	1 small cucumber

To prepare the appetizer: Bring one quart of water to a boil. Plunge the peaches into the water. After thirty seconds, remove the peaches and place them on a plate. Remove the skin from the peaches and cut them in half, from top (stem) to bottom. Remove the pits. In a large skillet, melt the butter or margarine. Saute the duck livers. Add the onion, the parsley, and the chopped egg; mix all well together with a wooden spoon. Add the garlic and the tarragon and season the whole to taste with salt and pepper. Reduce to medium heat for 5 to 10 minutes; then remove the liver mixture from the stove. Puree the mixture in a blender or food processor until very smooth. Transfer the puree to a pastry bag. Fill each peach half until all of the liver mixture is evenly distributed.

For service: Place the half peach in a lettuce cup. Garnish the top with julienne strips of the red pepper and the side of each plate with three or four thin slices of cucumber.

—Gideon Hirteinstein
Guest Services, Inc.
Washington, D.C.

Papaya Stuffed with Lox and Cream Cheese

serves four to eight

2 med. papaya
8 to 10 ounces lox
8 ounces cream cheese
1 green onion (chopped)
1 tsp parsley
1 tsp sweet paprika

1 TBSP garlic (minced)
1½ TBSP lemon juice
Salt and white pepper to taste
4 to 8 whole iceberg leaves
1 orange (sliced as half moons)

To prepare the appetizer: Peel the papaya and slice in half lengthwise. Remove the seeds. Slice each half in half also lengthwise. In a medium bowl, mix together the lox, the cream cheese, the green onion and the parsley. Purée in a blender or mixer until the mixture has a mousse-like consistency. Add the paprika, the garlic and the lemon. Season to taste with salt and pepper. Fill a pastry bag with the cream cheese and lox mixture. Fill each half papaya until the mixture is evenly distributed.

For service: Serve on individual serving plates with lettuce as a base and orange slices for garnish. Serve with crackers.

—Gideon Hirteinstein
Guest Services, Inc.
Washington, D.C.

Lump Backfin Crabmeat with Cucumbers and Salsa

serves eight

1½ lbs. ripe tomatoes	1 TBSP vinegar
1 poblano chile *or* 2 small	6 cucumbers
jalapeño chiles	Salt and pepper to taste
1 small red onion (diced)	2 lbs. lump backfin crabmeat

To prepare the appetizer: Plunge the cored tomatoes into boiling water for 30 seconds and then into ice water. Remove the skins from the tomatoes, split them in half, and remove the seeds. Chop the tomatoes into ½-inch cubes. Roast the chili over open flame or on an electric range element and then chill. Remove the skin and the seeds and finely dice the chile. Mix together the tomatoes, the chile, the diced red onion, and the vinegar. Season the salsa to taste with salt and pepper and chill. Peel and remove the seeds from the cucumbers. Cut the cucumbers into long thin strips. Gently pick through the crabmeat, removing any shell. Divide the julienne of cucumber equally amongst the eight chilled plates and place neatly around the border. Put a ring of the tomato salsa inside the cucumbers with the crab in the center. Serve immediately.

—Philip Delaplane
The Trellis
Williamsburg

Softshell Crabs and Lump Backfin Crabmeat with Sherry Wine Vinaigrette

serves eight

Dressing
1¼ cups peanut oil
6 TBSP sherry wine vinegar
2 TBSP soy sauce
1 scallion (thinly sliced)
2 TBSP red and green pepper
(fine diced)
¼ tsp black pepper

16 med. or small softshell crabs
(live)
1 lb. lump backfin crabmeat
1 large head Boston lettuce
2 TBSP lemon juice
Salt and pepper to taste

To prepare the dressing: Whip together all items for the dressing and chill.

To prepare the softshells: Dress the softshells (or have your fishmonger do it) and sprinkle with the lemon juice and salt and pepper. Over wood or charcoal, grill the softshells, shell side down first, for no more than 2½ minutes on each side. Chill the grilled crabs.

For service: Gently pick the lump crabmeat to remove any shells. Set the crab aside. Clean the Boston lettuce and place three to four leaves on each chilled plate. Place two softshells on each bed of Boston. Divide the crabmeat equally and place on top of the softshells. Dress each appetizer with 4 TBSP of the dressing and serve immediately.

—Philip Delaplane
The Trellis
Williamsburg

The Trellis Mushroom Pâté

serves six to eight

1 cup onion (finely chopped)
¼ lb. unsalted butter
1 lb. mushrooms (finely chopped)
1 garlic clove (minced)
¼ cup dry sherry
2 tsp salt
1 tsp chervil
¾ tsp rosemary

¼ tsp ground black pepper
1 cup cream cheese
  (room temperature)
3 large eggs (lightly beaten)
⅓ cup parsley (chopped)
2 cups spinach (cooked and chopped)
1½ cups walnuts (finely chopped)

To prepare the pâté: In a saucepan over medium heat, sauté the onion in the butter for 4 to 5 minutes. Add the mushrooms and the garlic and cook for five minutes. Add the sherry, the salt, the chervil, the rosemary and the pepper. Allow the mixture to cook slowly for 10 minutes. Transfer the mixture to a stainless steel mixing bowl and allow to cool somewhat. Preheat oven to 350 degrees F. In a separate bowl, combine the softened .cream cheese, the eggs, the parsley, the spinach and the walnuts. When thoroughly mixed, combine with the mushroom mixture. Butter a 1-quart loaf pan. Spoon the mixture into the pan. Cover the loaf pan with aluminum foil. Place the loaf pan in a larger and deeper pan partially filled with water. Bake the pâté for 1 hour and 15 minutes. After baking remove the loaf pan from the oven and the water pan. Cool the pâté inverted on a plate. When chilled the pâté may be removed from the loaf pan and sliced for service.

Serve slices of the pâté with sliced apples, toasted wheat bread, and a well chilled glass of Sauvignon Blanc.

—Marcel Desaulniers
The Trellis
Williamsburg

Over the years since I left home and lived in different cities, I have kept thinking about the people I grew up with and about our way of life. Whenever I go back to visit my sisters and brothers, we relive old times, remembering the past. And when we share again in gathering wild strawberries, canning, rendering lard, finding walnuts, picking persimmons, making fruitcake, I realize how much the bond that held us had to do with food.

—Edna Lewis
The Taste of Country Cooking, 1976

SALADS

*A Kitchin-Garden don't thrive better or
faster in any Part of the Universe, than
there. They have all the Culinary Plants
that grow in* England, *and in far greater
perfection, than in* England. *These they
dish up various ways, and find them very
delicious Sauce to their Meats, both Roast
and Boild, Fresh and Salt; such as the Red-
Buds, Sassafras-Flowers, Cymnels, Melons,
and Potatoes ...*

—Robert Beverly
*The History and Present
State of Virginia,* 1705

Tobacco Company House Dressing

serves eight

1½ cups mayonnaise
1⅛ tsp lemon juice
1⅛ tsp onion (minced)
½ tsp garlic powder *or*
   fresh minced garlic
½ tsp salt

2 tsp black pepper (coarsely ground)
1½ TBSP sugar
3 TBSP white vinegar
1⅛ tsp prepared yellow mustard
3 TBSP vegetable oil

To prepare the dressing: Blend the mayonnaise on low speed. Add the lemon juice, the onion, the salt, the garlic and the pepper. Continue blending. Add the sugar and blend. Add the vinegar and the mustard and blend. Add the oil, one TBSP at a time, blending well between each addition. The dressing will hold, covered, in refrigeration, for one week.

—Mark Kimmel
The Tobacco Company
Richmond

Seafood Salad Dressing

serves eight

2 cups sour cream
2 cups buttermilk
¼ cup onion (finely diced)
3 fresh garlic cloves (finely chopped)

4 fillets anchovies (finely chopped)
½ large lemon (juiced)
½ TBSP celery salt
½ TBSP Worcestershire sauce

To prepare the dressing: Combine the sour cream and the buttermilk in a blender. Add the chopped onions, the garlic, and the anchovies. Blend at low speed for 2 minutes. Add the lemon juice, the celery salt and the Worcestershire sauce. Blend again at medium speed for 2 minutes.

—Ted Kristensen
The Williamsburg Lodge
Williamsburg

Sauce Vinaigrette "Chef Paul"

serves eighteen

1 egg
¼ cup Dijon-style mustard
1½ cups white wine
1½ cups wine vinegar
1½ tsp salt
1½ tsp thyme leaves
¼ tsp ground white pepper
⅜ tsp oregano

½ tsp nutmeg
½ tsp rosemary
½ tsp basil
2 garlic cloves
2 cups vegetable oil
½ cup olive oil
1 cup water

To prepare the dressing: Very special care must be taken to mix as directed so that the dressing will not separate. Gather all the oils, wines, and spices. Separate the egg. In a blender, put the egg yolk, the mustard, the wine, the wine vinegar and the spices. Mix these ingredients well at medium speed for about 30 seconds and be careful not to turn the blender off. With the blender still moving, slowly add the oil, pouring it into the blender in a very thin stream. If the oil is added to quickly, the dressing will separate. Refrigerate the dressing after making.

—Paul Elbling
La Petite France
Richmond

Salade Vert-Pre

serves four

4 tomatoes
4 whole potatoes
2 eggs
4 fillets anchovies
3 branches parsley

1 lb. French cut green beans
  (cooked)
1 TBSP capers
Chef Paul's dressing (page 41)
1 head Boston lettuce

To prepare the salad: In a saucepan bring to a boil enough salted water to cover the tomatoes. Put the tomatoes in the water for 20 seconds. Remove them, and place in a bowl of cold water. Peel the tomatoes. Cut each tomato in half and scoop out the centers. Boil, peel and dice the potatoes. Hard boil and chop the eggs. Chop the anchovies and the parsley. Mix the potatoes, the eggs, the anchovies, the parsley, the capers and the green beans very well in a large bowl. Stuff the tomato halves with this mixture. Drizzle dressing over the stuffed tomatoes and serve on a large plate on a bed of Boston lettuce.

—Paul Elbling
La Petite France
Richmond

Marie-Antoinette

serves four

4 Belgian endive (very fresh)
8 branches watercress

6 fresh mushrooms
Chef Paul's dressing (page 41)

To prepare the salad: Break the endives and the watercress into bite-sized portions, but not too small. Toss the lettuces together with the thinly sliced mushrooms. Garnish all with Chef Paul's dressing.

—Paul Elbling
La Petite France
Richmond

Salad of Watercress, Cucumbers and Spinach with Walnut Oil and Raspberry Vinegar Dressing

serves eight

Dressing
½ cup raspberry vinegar
1 cup walnut oil
½ tsp salt
½ tsp black pepper
3 TBSP crème fraiche
    (page 134)

Salad
6 med. cucumbers
    (peeled and scored)
4 bunches watercress
2 heads Boston lettuce
30 to 40 leaves spinach
24 red raspberries
24 walnut halves

To prepare the dressing: Combine all ingredients and mix well.

To prepare the Salad: Core the cucumbers, and slice them into ¼-inch circles. Place the cucumbers in circles around the edges of eight 9-inch plates. Place sprigs of watercress through the center of each cucumber circle. Arrange a few leaves of Boston lettuce in center of plate, inside the ring of cucumbers. Place a few spinach leaves on top of the Boston lettuce. Dress each salad with 1½ ounces (three TBSP) of the dressing. Garnish each salad with three red raspberries and three walnut halves.

—Marcel Desaulniers
The Trellis
Williamsburg

Zucchini Salad

serves eight

1 cup white wine vinegar
¾ cup olive oil
2 TBSP sugar
1 tsp dried basil (*or* 1 TBSP fresh)
1 garlic clove (minced)

4 cups zucchini (sliced)
Leaf lettuce as needed
¼ cup green onion (sliced with tops)
2 med. tomatoes (thin wedges)

To prepare the dressing: In a screw-top jar, mix the vinegar, the oil, the sugar, the basil, the garlic, one teaspoon of salt and a few dashes of fresh ground pepper. Cover the jar and shake well.

43

To prepare the salad: Cook the zucchini in a small amount of boiling salted water until "crisp-tender," about 2 minutes, and drain. Arrange half the zucchini in one layer in a 10-by-6-by-2-inch dish. Shake the dressing to mix. Pour half of the dressing over the zucchini. Make another layer with the remaining zucchini and top with the remaining dressing. Cover the dish and *chill overnight.* To serve, drain the zucchini, reserving ¼ cup of the dressing. Arrange the zucchini on a lettuce-lined plate. Arrange the green onion on top of the zucchini. Arrange the tomatoes around the zucchini and drizzle with the reserved dressing. Chill before serving if desired.

—Art Cook
The Westwood Racquet Club
Richmond

Endive Belge Vinaigrette Mimosa

serves eight

Dressing
¾ cup vegetable oil
½ cup wine vinegar
1 TBSP Dijon-style mustard
1 garlic clove (mashed)
2 TBSP herbs (parsley, thyme,
    marjoram, tarragon)
Salt and pepper to taste

Endive
8 Belgian endive
Leaf lettuce as needed

Mimosa topping
½ cup bread crumbs
2 TBSP butter
1 egg (hard-cooked and chopped)
1 TBSP fresh parsley (chopped)
Salt and pepper to taste

To prepare the dressing: Mix all ingredients well.

To prepare the endive: Cut the endive in quarters and marinate in the dressing for 2 to 3 hours.

To prepare the Mimosa: Sauté the bread crumbs in butter until crisp and light brown. Add the chopped hard-cooked egg and the parsley and season with salt and pepper.

For service: Place the quartered endives on individual plates on a bed of leaf lettuce and top with the Mimosa.

—Richard J. Nelson
Richmond

44

Chicken Salad Imperial

serves four

8 ounces chicken breast
  (poached and diced)
2 large stalks celery (diced)
½ med. onion (finely diced)

1 cup mayonnaise
1 pinch celery salt
Salt and pepper to taste
2 med. ripe papayas

To prepare the salad: Combine the diced chicken, the celery, the onion, and the mayonnaise. Mix well. Season to taste with salt and pepper. Split the papayas lengthwise; scoop out the seeds. Fill the hollow with chicken salad. Serve the papayas on a platter with lettuce. Garnish them with sliced pineapple and radishes.

—Ted Kristensen
The Williamsburg Lodge
Williamsburg

Tropicale Salad with Curried Chutney Dressing

serves eight

Dressing
4½ TBSP sugar
¼ tsp salt
1 TBSP cornstarch
½ cup pineapple juice
2 TBSP lemon juice
2 eggs (well-beaten)
5 ounces (10 TBSP) cream cheese
  (room temperature)
⅛ tsp curry powder
¼ cup chutney (finely chopped)

4 small heads romaine lettuce
Mandarin orange slices for garnish
Sliced almonds for garnish
Whole wheat croutons for garnish

To prepare the dressing: Combine the sugar, the salt, and the cornstarch. Add the pineapple and lemon juice. Cook over low heat, stirring constantly until the mixture is thick and bubbly. Continue cooking and stirring for 2 minutes or until the mixture is smooth. Beat the eggs in a separate bowl. Add a small amount of the hot mixture to the eggs and blend well. Continue to add the hot mixture to the eggs in very small

45

amounts until the eggs are heated through. Add the egg mixture to the remaining hot custard. Cook for 2 to 3 minutes longer. Cool the custard by placing the saucepan in a cold water bath. Whip the cream cheese until fluffy. Slowly beat the cooked custard into the cream cheese. Add the curry and the chutney. Blend until smooth.

For service: Toss a small amount of the dressing with romaine lettuce, adding more dressing as desired. Serve on a well-chilled plate, topped with the mandarin orange slices, the almonds and the croutons.

—Mark Kimmel
The Tobacco Company
Richmond

Hot Curried Fruit Salad

serves six to eight

4 fresh pears *or* 1 16-ounce can
  (peeled, cored, and quartered)
1 16-ounce can apricots
1 pineapple *or* 1 16-ounce can
  (peeled, and cut into chunks)
4 fresh peaches *or* 1 16-ounce can
  (peeled and cut into chunks)

4 ripe bananas (sliced diagonally and
  soaked in fruit juice)
1 tsp. light rum
6 TBSP unsalted butter
¼ cup brown sugar
2 tsp. curry powder
Toasted slivered almonds
  for garnish

To prepare the salad: Preheat oven to 350 degrees F. Reserve one half cup of fruit juice. Mix the fruit juice with the light rum. In a saucepan combine this mixture with the butter, the brown sugar, and the curry powder. Cook on medium heat until bubbly and brown and set aside. Place the fruit in a casserole or ovenproof serving dish. Pour the sauce over the fruit and bake, uncovered, for 1 hour. Garnish the finished salad with toasted almonds before serving.

—Dominador Valeros
Virginia Beach Yacht Club
Virginia Beach

Asparagus Vinaigrette

serves four to six

¼ cup cider vinegar
2 TBSP pommerey mustard
¾ cup olive oil
2 TBSP red onion (finely diced)
2 TBSP parsley (finely chopped)

1 tsp fresh dill *or* tarragon
(finely chopped)
1 to 1½ lbs. fresh asparagus
Salt and pepper to taste

To prepare the dressing: Whisk the vinegar and the mustard together. Very slowly add the olive oil. Add the onion and the fresh herbs. Season the dressing to taste. Chill the dressing at least 2 hours before serving. It is best if made the day before.

To prepare the asparagus: Lightly peel the asparagus with a vegetable parer. In boiling salted water cook the asparagus until just tender (about 1 minute). Immediately plunge the asparagus into ice water. Dress and serve chilled.

—Lisa Pittman
The Williamsburg Inn
Williamsburg

Salad of Spring Greens

serves four

Dressing
1 cup extra-virgin olive oil
2 shallots (minced)
½ cup fresh herbs (basil, dill,
chives, parsley, garlic tops,
coriander, etc.)
1 TBSP balsamic vinegar
Salt and fresh ground pepper
to taste

Greens
(almost any spring greens can
be substituted)
2 cups soft spring lettuce
(loosely packed)
2 cups young spinach
(loosely packed)
½ cup mustard greens
(loosely packed)
½ cup garden cress
4 mustard flowers

To prepare the dressing: Slowly pour the olive oil into a blender or food processor containing the shallots, the mustard greens, and the herbs.

Process on high. Remove the mixture to a bowl. Stir in the vinegar. Season the dressing to taste with the salt and fresh ground pepper. Refrigerate *at least 24 hours.*

To prepare the salad: Wash the greens well in cold water. Arrange in concentric circles from the outside of the individual plates: the lettuce, the spinach, the mustard and the cress. Dress the greens. Garnish each plate with a flavorful mustard flower.

—Jonathan A. Zearfoss
The Trellis
Williamsburg

Frühling (Spring) Salad

serves eight

Dressing
¾ cup olive oil
⅛ cup cider vinegar
⅛ cup sherry wine vinegar
2 shallots (peeled and minced)
Salt and white pepper to taste

2 boneless duck breasts (skin on)
8 mushrooms (washed, stemmed, sliced)

Lettuces
(amounts must be estimated)
spinach leaves
dandelion leaves
radicchio rosso (red leaf)
lambs lettuce

To prepare the dressing: Make the dressing in advance by mixing all of the ingredients thoroughly. Allow the dressing to stand at room temperature.

To prepare the duck breast: Preheat oven to 350 degrees F. In a hot skillet sauté both sides of the duck breasts. Bake the breasts until medium rare, about 3 to 4 minutes. Pink must still be visible when the breasts are sliced. Remove the duck from the oven and allow to cool at room temperature.

To prepare the salad: Prepare the greens by removing stems and washing gently in a large amount of cool water. Remove the greens from the water and drain them. Arrange the greens on plates. Slice the duck breast, thinly and on a bias, just before serving. Arrange the duck and the thinly sliced mushrooms on the greens. Top with the dressing. Serve immediately.

—Rhys Lewis
The Williamsburg Inn
Williamsburg

Tuna Salad with Sour Fruit

serves four

1 6½-ounce-can tuna
1 med. sour apple (grated)
1 hard peach (large grated)
1 small mango (grated)
3 TBSP sour cream
2 TBSP mayonnaise
1 TBSP lemon juice

1 TBSP orange zest
1 tsp dill
Salt and pepper to taste
4 leaves iceberg lettuce
1 carrot (grated fine)
1 lemon (wedged)

To prepare the salad: Drain the tuna of water or oil. Gently break apart the tuna with fingers into a medium bowl. Add the grated apple, peach, and mango. Add the sour cream, the mayonnaise, the lemon juice, the orange zest and the dill. Mix gently, seasoning to taste with the salt and pepper. Chill.

For service: Just before serving place a lettuce leaf on each of the individual plates. Portion the salad. Garnish the top with grated carrot and the side of the plate with a wedge of lemon.

—Gideon Hirteinstein
Guest Services, Inc.
Washington, D.C.

Jeff's Potato Salad

serves six to eight

6 med. white potatoes
1 med. red onion (diced)
3 stalks celery (diced)
¼ lb. country ham (diced)
1 quart water
Salt and pepper to taste

Dressing
1½ cups mayonnaise
2 tsp Dijon-style mustard
1 tsp cider vinegar
2 tsp sugar
¼ tsp celery seed

To prepare the salad: In a medium pot cook the potatoes in one quart of salted water for 30 minutes or until done. While the potatoes are cooking, prepare the vegetables and the dressing. To make the dressing, combine all of the ingredients. When done, cool the potatoes; then peel and dice. In a large bowl combine all of the ingredients. Season to taste with salt and pepper. Serve chilled.

—Jeff Duncan
The Trellis
Williamsburg

Root Vegetables with Chicken Breast

serves four

2 chicken breasts (poached)
1 parsnip
1 celery root
1 med. carrot
1 stalk celery
1 small turnip
3 TBSP mayonnaise
1½ TBSP ketchup
½ tsp Worcestershire sauce

1 tsp garlic (chopped)
1 tsp lemon juice
1 tsp white vinegar
Salt and white pepper to taste
4 to 5 leaves watercress
2 tomatoes (sliced)
1 cucumber (sliced)
1 egg (hard-cooked)
1 tsp parsley (chopped)

To prepare the salad: Remove all skin from the cooled chicken breasts. Slice the breasts into very long and thin strips. Place the chicken meat in a medium bowl. Wash and dry the vegetables. Lightly peel the parsnip and the carrot. Peel the celery root and the turnip. Slice all the vegetables into a very thin julienne. Add the vegetables to the bowl of chicken. Add the mayonnaise, the ketchup, the Worcestershire, the garlic, the lemon juice, and the vinegar. Mix gently being careful not to break up the vegetables. Season to taste with the salt and pepper. Chill.

For service: Place watercress leaves on the individual plates. Distribute the salad equally. On one side of the plate, lay the slices of tomato. On the other side lay the cucumber. Top the salad with a slice of egg. Sprinkle with parsley.

—Gideon Hirteinstein
Guest Services, Inc.
Washington, D.C.

Crabmeat Salad Tropicana

serves six to eight

1 lb. fresh backfin crabmeat
1 med. mango (peeled and julienned)
1 cup fresh pineapple (cubed)
1 small papaya (cubed)
5 TBSP mayonnaise
½ lemon (juiced)

½ orange (skin, zested)
Salt and pepper to taste
8 cups iceberg lettuce
2 med. oranges (sliced)
1 cucumber (sliced)
2 tsp parsley (chopped)

To prepare the salad: In a medium bowl, combine the picked crabmeat, the mango, the pineapple and the papaya. Add the mayonnaise, the lemon juice, and the orange zest. Mix slowly by hand, seasoning to taste with the salt and pepper. Chill for 1 hour.

For service: On individual salad plates, place lettuce cups. Distribute the salad equally to each cup. Garnish with orange and cucumber slices on the plate. Sprinkle chopped parsley on top.

—Gideon Hirteinstein
Guest Services, Inc.
Washington, D.C.

Israelien Avocado Salad

serves four

2 med. avocados	1½ TBSP feta cheese
1 tomato (small cubes)	2 TBSP lemon juice
1 green onion (chopped)	1 tsp garlic (minced)
1 cucumber (peeled and cubed)	Salt and white pepper to taste
1 small red pepper (diced)	4 iceberg leaves
3 TBSP cottage cheese	1 whole orange (half moon slices)
1½ TBSP sour cream	1 TBSP parsley (chopped)

To prepare the salad: Wash and dry all the vegetables. Remove the skin from the avocados. Split the avocados in half lengthwise and remove the seeds. Cut the avocados into cubes. Put the avocados in a medium bowl. Add the tomato, the green onion, the cucumber, and the red bell pepper. Add the cottage cheese, the sour cream, and the feta cheese. Add the lemon and the garlic. Mix slowly. Season to taste with the salt and pepper.

For service: Just before serving, place the lettuce leaves on individual plates. Portion the salad equally. Garnish the border with orange slices. Sprinkle with chopped parsley. Serve chilled.

—Gideon Hirteinstein
Guest Services, Inc.
Washington, D.C.

1794.
Objects for the garden and farm

Peas. Charlton
    Marrow-fat
    green for soup.
Beans. Windsor, brown,
    Lima
    Mazareen
    Alleghaney
    Snap.
Cabbage
Cauliflower
Broccoli
turnips
carrots
parsneps
Jerusalem artichoke.
Indian potato
beet.
salsafia
horse radish.
peendars

Lettuce. cabbage
    Cos.
    longleaved.
Endive. curled
    winter
radishes.
celery solid
parsley
spinach
cresses mountn.
nasturtium
sorrel French
shalots
leeks.
garlick
onions
white mustard
cucumb. forw.
    long green

squashes
potato pumpk.
melons citron
    pineapple
    green
    Venice
    Water
strawberries
gooseberries
currans
vines Malesherb.
artichokes
pomegran.
figs.
hops.

Objects for the garden and farm

sage
balm
mint
thyme.
lavender
marjoram
camomile
tansey
rue
wormwood
southernwood
rosemary
hyssop
perywinkle
marshmellow
beargrass.

Lilac.
jasmine white yellow
honeysuckle.
althaea
gelder rose
dble bloss almond
red maple
Lombardy poplar
Balsam poplar
Weeping willow
Willow oak
Groud oak
Kentuckey coffee
Missouri Laurus
Paccan. furze.
Spanish broom
Calycanthus
roses

Lucern
St. foin
Burnet
red clover
white clover
white bent grass.
corn. forwd yellow.
Mars.'s
    forwd white
Indian peas. French
Wild pea
horsebean.
buckwheat
Irish potato
Spring wheat
Dry rice

—*Thomas Jefferson's Garden Book*, 1766-1824

Romaine Lettuce and Red Bartlett Pears
with Hazelnut Vinaigrette

serves eight

6 ounces hazelnuts (toasted,
skins removed, split)
8 red Bartlett pears
1¼ cups vegetable oil

6 TBSP raspberry vinegar
2 heads romaine lettuce
Salt and pepper to taste

To prepare the dressing: Purée one third of the hazelnuts and one peeled and cored pear with the vegetable oil and the vinegar. Season to taste with salt and pepper. Chill.

To prepare the salad: Clean the romaine, saving the larger leaves for the base of the salad and slicing the smaller. Quarter each pear (do not peel) and remove the core. Slice each quartered pear four times lengthwise. Assemble the salad on chilled plates. Place four to six leaves on each plate, the chopped romaine in the middle, and the sliced pears around the edge of the chopped romaine. Emulsify the dressing and spoon over the salads. Sprinkle each salad with split hazelnuts and serve.

—Philip Delaplane
The Trellis
Williamsburg

Curly Endive, Potatoes and
Fresh Corn with Bacon Dressing

serves eight

Dressing
1½ cups vegetable oil
½ cup cider vinegar
Salt and pepper to taste

2 med. heads curly endive (chicory)
1 lb. red bliss potatoes
3 ears fresh sweet corn
½ lb. bacon (smoked slab
if available)

To prepare the dressing: Whip together the dressing ingredients and chill.

To prepare the salad: Blanch the potatoes in boiling, salted water until just done, about 12 to 15 minutes. Plunge the cooked potatoes into ice water. When the potatoes are cool, drain and cut them into quarters. Blanch the cleaned corn in boiling, salted water for 2 minutes and remove to an ice bath. When cool, cut the whole kernels from the ear and hold chilled. Trim and cut the bacon into ¼-inch cubes. Cook the bacon over medium heat until crisp. Remove and drain on a towel. Reserve the bacon fat in the pan. Clean the chicory and divide equally amongst chilled plates. Raise the heat under the bacon fat to medium high. When hot, carefully add the potatoes and cook until light brown. Remove the potatoes and drain on a towel.

For service: Put the warm potatoes on the lettuce. Distribute the corn over the potatoes. Dress each salad with four TBSP of dressing. Sprinkle with bacon and serve.

—Philip Delaplane
The Trellis
Williamsburg

Don't after Foreign Food and Clothing roam,
But learn to eat and wear what's rais'd at Home.
Kind Nature suits each Clime with what it wants,
Sufficient to subsist th' Inhabitants.

—Benjamin Franklin

Romaine and Avocado with Hickory Smoked Cheddar and "Caesar" Mayonnaise

serves four

Dressing
2 egg yolks
2 TBSP lemon juice
1 cup olive oil
½ tsp Worcestershire sauce
½ tsp dry mustard
2 to 4 anchovies
2 large garlic cloves
½ tsp tabasco
1 small shallot (minced)

2 tsp freshly ground pepper
½ tsp salt
4 TBSP red wine vinegar

2 heads young romaine lettuce
2 ripe avocados (peeled and
    cut into ¾-inch cubes)
¼ lb. hickory smoked cheddar
    (¼-inch cubes)
Croutons (if desired)

To prepare the dressing: In a clean stainless steel bowl, with a clean whip, whisk the egg yolks with the lemon until slightly thickened and a lighter shade of yellow. Line a bowl which will not spin with a kitchen towel. Setting the mixing bowl upon the towel, slowly add the oil to the egg yolks, whipping constantly, being sure that the mixture emulsifies constantly. Do not stop whipping until all of the oil is consumed. The mixture will be quite thick. Mash the Worcestershire, the mustard, the anchovies, the garlic, the tabasco and the minced shallots together to make a paste. Stir this paste into the mayonnaise. Add the pepper and the salt. Add the vinegar. If the dressing is too thick add water.

To prepare the salad: Clean and then tear the romaine into bite-sized pieces. Place in a large wooden bowl. Add the avocadoes, the cheese and the croutons. Pour the dressing over the top. Toss the salad with wooden spoons thirteen times. Serve immediately.

—Jonathan A. Zearfoss
The Trellis
Williamsburg

56

ENTRÉES

"At length from everie hutt in the towne, the women and old men brought forth the sundrie dishes of the feast, that had been some daies preparing. To each of us was given a platter of divers foods, and onelie one, wch shew'd, though it was sufficient to fill us with comfort, that none of us were reckon'd as contenders, save onelie Burlingame & Attonce, before whom they set dish after dish. For houres thereafter, while that the rest watch'd in astonishment, the two gluttons match'd dish for dish, and herewith is the summe of what they eat:

Of keskowghnoughmass, the yellow-belly'd sunne-fish,
    tenne apiece.
Of copatone, the sturgeon, one apiece.
Of pummahumpnoughmass, fry'd starfish, three apiece.
Of pawpeconoughmass, pype-fishes, four apiece, dry'd.
Of boyl'd froggs, divers apiece, assorted bulles, greenes,
    trees, & spring peepers.
Of blowfish, two apiece, frizzl'd & blow'd.
Of terrapin, a tortoise, one apiece, stew'd.

Also oysters, crabbs, trowt, croakers, rock-fish, flownders, clamms, maninose, & such other sea-food as they great Baye doth give up. They next did eate:

Of mallard, canvas-backe, & buffle-head ducks, morsels & mix'd
    peeces in like amounts.
Of hooded mergansers, one apiece, on picks as is there wont.
Of pypers, one apiece, dry'd & pouder'd.
Of cohunk, a taystie goose, half apiece.
Of snypes, one apiece, bagg'd.
Of black & white warblers, one apiece, throttl'd.
Of rubie-throated humming-birds, two apiece, scalded,
    pickl'd, & intensify'd.

Of gross-beeks, one apiece, bill'd and crack'd.
Of browne creepers, one apiece, hitt.
Of long-bill'd marsh wrenns., a bird, one apiece, growsl'd
   & disembowell'd.
Of catt birds, one apiece, dyc'd & fetch'd.
Of grows a legg apiece, smother'd naturall.

Also divers eggs, and bitts & bytes of turkie and what all. The fowles
done, they turn'd to meat, and eat:

Of marsh ratts, one apiece, fry'd.
Of raccoon, half a one apiece, grutted.
Of dogg, equal portions, a sort of spaniell it was.
Of venison, one pryme apiece, dry'd.
Of beare-cubb, a rasher each, roasted.
Of catamount, a haunch & griskin apiece, spitted and turn'd.
Of batts, two apiece, boyl'd, de gustibus & cet.

No rabbits. While that they eat of these severall meats, there were
serv'd to them vegetables, to the number of five: beanes, rockahominy
(wch is to say, parch'd & pouder'd mayze), eggplant (that the French
call aubergine), wild ryce, & a sallet of green reedes, that was call'd
Attaskus. Also berries of divers sorts, but no frute, and the whole
wash'd downe with glue-broth and greate draughts of Sawwehone-
suckhanna, wch signifyeth, bloudwater, a mild spirits they distill out
in the swamp.

—John Barth
"John Smith's Secret Historie"
The Sot-Weed Factor, 1960

FISH AND SEAFOOD

Of Fishe

There are also *Troutes, Porpoises, Rayes, Oldwives, Mullets, Plaice,* and very many other sortes of excellent good fishe, which we haue taken & eaten...There are also in many places plentie of these kinds which follow.

Sea crabbes, such as we haue in England. *Oystres,* some very great, and some small; some rounde and some of a long shape: They are founde both in salt water and brackish, and those that we had out of salt water are far better than the other as in our owne countrey.

Also *Muscles, Scalopes, Periwinkles* and *Oreuises.*

Seekanauk, a kind of crustie shell fishe which is good meate, about a foote in breadth, hauing a crustie tayle, many legges like a crab; and her eyes in her backe. They are founde in shallowes of salt waters; and sometime on the shoare.

There are many *Tortoyses* both of lande and sea kinde, their backs & bellies are shelled very thicke; their head, feete, and taile, which are in appearance, seeme ougly as though they were membres of a serpent or venomous: but notwithstanding they are very good meate as also their egges. Some haue bene founde of a yard in bredth and better.

And thus haue I made relation of all sortes of victuall that we fed vpon for the time we were in *Virginia*...as farre foorth as I knowe and can remember or that are specially worthy to bee remembred.

—Thomas Hariot
A briefe and true report..., 1588

Flounder Walewska

serves four

Lobster mousse
¾ lb. lobster tails (frozen)
8 ounces bay shrimp (frozen)
1 cup heavy cream
10 eggs (beaten)
4 TBSP flour
Salt and pepper to taste

Sherburg sauce
1 quart white sauce (see index)
1 TBSP butter
2 cups mushrooms (sliced)
2 TBSP white wine
½ cup Parmesan cheese
(freshly grated)

4 6-ounce fillets flounder
1 cup water
1 cup white wine
Whole peppercorns to taste
Dill to taste

To prepare the mousse: Defrost the lobster meat and the shrimp. Put all of the ingredients for the mousse in a blender or food processor and process at medium speed for 4 minutes.

To prepare the sauce: To one quart of white sauce, add the mushrooms sautéed in butter, the white wine, and the Parmesan cheese.

To prepare the flounder: Fill a wide pan with water, one cup of white wine, whole peppercorns and dill. Bring the liquid to a boil, then reduce the heat until the liquid is barely moving. Place two TBSP of the lobster mousse two inches from the end of each flounder fillet and roll the fillet. Poach the flounder in the liquid for 10 to 15 minutes. Remove the fish and drain. Place on serving platter and cover with Sherburg sauce.
    Serve the flounder with rice or steamed parsleyed potatoes.

—Ted Kristensen
The Williamsburg Lodge
Williamsburg

Scallops Lafayette

serves four

6 TBSP butter
1 small onion (diced)
½ green pepper (diced)
12 mushrooms (sliced)
2 lbs. scallops (bay or sea)
Salt and pepper to taste

1 TBSP lemon juice
1 TBSP sherry
8 tomato slices
8 wedges avocado
4 TBSP Parmesan cheese (grated)

To prepare the scallops: Preheat oven to 375 degrees F. In a large sauté pan, melt the butter. Sauté the onion, the green pepper, and the mushrooms. Add the scallops and season to taste with the salt and pepper. Add the lemon and the sherry. Place the mixture in a small casserole and top with the tomato slices and the avocado. Sprinkle with the Parmesan. Bake the scallops for 10 minutes. Garnish with fresh chopped parsley.

—Richard J. Nelson
Richmond

Sautéed Softshell Crabs with Madiera-Pinenut Butter Sauce

serves four

Butter sauce
¼ shallot (peeled, very
　finely minced)
¼ cup pinenuts (well-chopped,
　but not pureed)
1 cup Madiera
2 cups (4 sticks) butter, divided

8 softshell crabs (or 12 if
　they are small)
½ cup flour, seasoned with
　salt and pepper
2 TBSP peanut oil

To prepare the butter sauce: Sauté the shallots and the pinenuts in a sauté pan with one TBSP of butter. Add the Madeira (the better the Madeira, the better the sauce). Reduce over medium heat by sixty percent. Remove the skillet from direct heat and slowly add the butter in two TBSP increments, whipping constantly. It is important to keep a constant lukewarm temperature or either the sauce will not emulsify or the butter will separate. As soon as the butter is incorporated, transfer the sauce to a crock and hold warm near the range, but allow no direct heat.

To prepare the crabs: Clean the crabs or have your fishmonger do it. Dredge the crabs in the seasoned flour. Heat the oil in a sauté pan to medium high. Place the crabs in the skillet underside up. Sauté until the shell is reddish-brown, but no longer than 3 minutes. Turn the crabs and sauté the underside, but *do not crisp*, allow no more than 2 minutes.

For service: Flood dinner plates with the sauce, placing two (or three) softshells in the center. Garnish with toasted pinenuts.

—Mike Rollins, apprentice
Colonial Williamsburg

Crab Norfolk

serves four

¾ cup dry white wine
1 tsp lemon juice
2 shallots (minced)
6 TBSP sweet butter
(room temperature)

½ cup rich fish stock
2 lbs. crab meat (picked to
remove shell)
1 TBSP parsley (fresh chopped)
Salt and pepper to taste

To prepare the crab: Reduce the white wine and the lemon juice by half in a sauté pan. Lower the heat and add the minced shallots. Add the softened butter, bit by bit. It is very important to swirl the pan constantly or stir with a wire whisk to melt the butter without allowing it to separate. Add the fish stock and continue to whisk. Add the crabmeat and finish with the parsley. Season to taste with salt and pepper. Serve in a casserole or serving dish with croutons fried in butter.

—Dominador Valeros
Virginia Beach Yacht Club
Virginia Beach

Stuffed Soft Shell Crabs Supreme
with Gloucester Sauce

serves six

Stuffing
1 lb. backfin crabmeat
2 tsp green pepper (diced)
1 tsp onion (diced)
2 tsp Dijon-style mustard
¼ tsp Old Bay seasoning
½ tsp lemon juice
½ tsp white pepper
½ tsp celery salt
3 TBSP sour cream
8 saltines (crushed)
4 tsp flour
4 egg whites

Sauce
6 eggs (beaten)
½ cup sour cream
1 tsp lemon juice
1 tsp Old Bay seasoning
¼ tsp paprika

6 hotel prime softshell crabs
1 cup flour
1 tsp Old Bay seasoning
Clarified butter *or* vegetable oil
(as needed)

To prepare the stuffing: Pick the crabmeat to remove shell. Combine all of the stuffing ingredients except the egg whites and the crabmeat. Mix well. Beat the egg whites until fluffy. Blend the egg whites together with

64

the other ingredients. Fold in the crabmeat gently being careful not to break up the large pieces of crabmeat.

To prepare the sauce: Combine all ingredients. Mix.

To prepare the crabs: Preheat oven to 325 degrees F. Clean the crabs or have your fishmonger do it. Combine the flour and the one tsp of Old Bay. Dredge the crabs lightly in this mixture. Pan fry the softshells in clarified butter until golden brown. Fill the top of each softshell with the stuffing mixture. Move the crabs to a baking pan and cover all with Gloucester Sauce. Bake for ½ hour or until golden brown.

—Bill Pearce
Pearce's Parties
Richmond

Crab Vanderbilt

serves four

1 med. pimento drained *or*
   1 med. red bell pepper
½ med. green pepper
½ med. onion
1 lb. Alaskan Snow crabmeat
1 small bay leaf
1 TBSP butter

1½ cups Mornay sauce (see index)
¼ tsp salt
¼ tsp white pepper
4 tsp white wine
4 tsp brandy
8 asparagus spears *or*
   broccoli florets

To prepare the crab: Dice the pimento or red bell pepper, the green pepper, and the onion. Reserve four large pieces of crabmeat. Shred the remainder of the crab. Sauté the peppers, the onion, and the bay leaf in butter until the vegetables are "crisp tender." Add the shredded crabmeat and the mornay sauce. Bring the mixture to a simmer. Add the salt and the pepper and continue to simmer, stirring occasionally, for 8 to 10 minutes. Add the wine and the brandy and mix well. Remove from the heat and serve. Top each serving with one piece of the reserved crabmeat and two pieces of the asparagus or the broccoli.

—Mark Kimmel
The Tobacco Company
Richmond

> *Fish and visitors smell in three days.*
>
> —Benjamin Franklin

Crabmeat Raphael

serves four

Sauce
1 28-ounce can Italian-style
   whole tomatoes with juice
2 small onions (coarsely chopped)
¼ cup parsley (fresh chopped fine)
2 med. garlic cloves (minced)
3 TBSP olive oil
   (at room temperature)
2 TBSP basil leaves (dried)
¼ tsp oregano
¼ tsp salt

½ cup grated Romano cheese
½ tsp black pepper (coarsely ground)
¾ tsp crushed red pepper

1 lb. fresh crabmeat
¾ lb. fresh pasta (preferably
vermicelli *or* other fine pasta)
   or, 1 lb. pasta (imported, dried)
3 quarts water
1½ TBSP olive oil
¾ TBSP salt

To prepare the sauce: In a bowl, crush the tomatoes. Chop the onions and the parsley. Mince the garlic. Combine all of the ingredients for the sauce. Simmer over low heat for 30 minutes, stirring occasionally. DO NOT allow the sauce to boil as it will lose its bright appearance and fresh flavor. The sauce can be refrigerated for up to five days at this point.

One hour before service, pick the crabmeat to remove cartilage. Heat the sauce to a simmer slowly to prevent scorching. As the sauce begins to simmer, start water for the pasta, adding 1½ TBSP olive oil and ¾ TBSP salt.

For fresh pasta: Add the crabmeat to the sauce and stir until the crab is heated through, about 1½ minutes. Cook the pasta for 30 seconds. Drain immediately. Add the sauce and toss together. Serve immediately.

For dried pasta: Cook the pasta according to package instructions for al dente. When 1½ to 2 minutes of cooking time remain, add the crabmeat to the sauce and stir until heated through, about 1½ minutes. Drain the pasta, add to it the sauce, and toss together. Serve immediately.

—Mark Kimmel
The Tobacco Comapny
Richmond

Fillet of Salmon with Lump Crabmeat, Asparagus and Pistachios

serves eight

16 stalks asparagus (peeled)
¼ lb. pistachios (shelled,
  skinned, crushed)
8 4- to 6-ounce salmon fillets
4 TBSP lemon juice

¼ cup flour (seasoned)
6 TBSP unsalted butter, divided
1 lb. lump backfin crabmeat
  (picked to remove shell)
Salt and pepper to taste

To prepare the salmon: Blanch the asparagus for 40 seconds in boiling salted water. Remove and plunge immediately into ice water. Cut the asparagus on a bias into ¾-inch pieces and reserve. Prepare the pistachios, which should yield about ½ cup. Marinate the salmon in the lemon juice. Dust the salmon fillets lightly with flour, patting to remove excess. Preheat oven to 350 F. In a large oven-safe sauté pan, melt one TBSP butter. Sauté four of the salmon fillets for 1 minute on each side. Remove the fillets to a plate and melt another TBSP of butter. Sauté the other four fillets. Return all the salmon portions to the pan and finish in the oven for 5 to 7 minutes or until the flesh just becomes opaque. Meanwhile, melt the remaining four TBSP of butter in a sauté pan on medium high heat. Sauté the asparagus for 1 minute. Season lightly. Add the crabmeat and sauté until just hot, seasoning to taste with the salt and pepper.

For service: Plate the salmon portions. Top with the crabmeat mixture. Sprinkle pistachios over the top of the crabmeat. Serve with lemon.

—Jonathan A. Zearfoss
The Trellis
Williamsburg

Indonesian Shrimp Sauté

serves four

Marinade
½ cup plus 1 TBSP pimentoes
  (with juice)
¼ cup plus 2 TBSP vegetable oil
¾ TBSP red wine vinegar
2 to 3 garlic cloves (crushed)

1 tsp salt
1½ tsp crushed red pepper
¾ tsp cumin

1 lb. (21 to 25 ct.) shrimp
½ lb. carrots (peeled and julienned)
½ lb. snow pea pods

To prepare the marinade: Purée all of the marinade ingredients in a food processor or blender. Clean and devein the shrimp. Place the shrimp in a plastic or glass container. Pour the marinade over them. Toss to coat the shrimp. Marinate for 2 to 6 hours.

For service: Half an hour before service, pare the carrots. Julienne to ⅛-by-2-inch strips. String the snow peas from both ends. Drain the shrimp but do not dry. Sauté the shrimp in the small amount of marinade that clings to them for 5 to 6 minutes. Add the carrots and the snow peas and sauté for 1 to 2 minutes more, until the vegetables are "crisp-tender." Serve over wild rice.

—Mark Kimmel
The Tobacco Company
Richmond

Seafood Sauté à la India

serves six

½ cup (1 stick) butter
1 med. tomato (diced)
1 sour apple (julienned)
2 green onions (chopped)
1 lb. baby shrimp
1 lb. fresh sea scallops
8 ounces flounder (julienned)
2 tsp curry powder
1 whole lemon (juiced)

1 tsp garlic (fresh chopped)
1 tsp mustard
1 tsp sugar
Salt and pepper to taste

Garnish
1 red apple (thin julienned)
2 tsp parsley (fresh chopped)

To prepare the sauté: In a large sauté pan, melt the butter. Add the tomato, the sour apple, and the green onion. Sauté for 3 to 4 minutes. Add the seafood. Mix gently, being careful not to break up the julienne strips. Add all of the spices. Mix gently, cover the pan, and simmer on *low* heat for 7 to 10 minutes. Remove the pan from the heat. Serve immediately.

For service: Divide the sautéed seafood into six casserole dishes. Sprinkle the top with the julienned red apple and the parsley. Serve with white rice.

—Gideon Hirteinstein
Guest Services, Inc.
Washington, D.C.

Brook Trout with Shrimp, Apples, Walnuts and Cream

serves eight

1 qt. heavy cream
8 fresh brook trout
   (boned, 8 to 10 ounces each)
6 TBSP olive oil
3 TBSP lemon juice

3 TBSP butter
1 lb. shrimp (peeled, deveined)
4 apples (cored, sliced)
Salt and pepper to taste
6 ounces walnuts (toasted)

To prepare the trout: In a heavy saucepot, bring the cream to a boil and then simmer until the volume is reduced by half. Hold the reduced cream warm. Trim the fins and head from the boned trout. Dip the trout in olive oil and lemon juice. Grill the fish over wood or charcoal for 7 to 8 minutes (or bake in a 350 degrees F. oven for 8 to 10 minutes). Melt the butter in a large sauté pan. Sauté the shrimp and the apples until done, on medium high, 2 to 4 minutes depending on the size of the shrimp. Season to taste with salt and pepper.

For service: Ladle two ounces of cream onto each plate. Place the trout on the plates. Top the trout with the shrimp and apples. Finish the plate with toasted walnuts and serve.

—Philip Delaplane
The Trellis
Williamsburg

Sautéed Snapper with Crabmeat, Mustard Grains and Chive Sauce

serves four

¼ cup heavy cream
1 pint white wine
Cracked black pepper to taste
1 tsp shallots (minced), divided
1 garlic clove (minced)
¼ tsp thyme
1 bay leaf
2 lemons (juiced), divided

4 cups plus 4 TBSP butter
1 tsp Dijon-style mustard
1 TBSP chives (chopped), divided
1 lime (juiced)
4 snapper fillets (skin removed)
Seasoned flour as needed
½ lb. lump backfin crabmeat

To prepare the sauce: Combine the heavy cream, the white wine, a pinch of freshly cracked black pepper, ½ tsp shallots, the garlic, the thyme, the bay leaf, and the juice of one lemon. Simmer the mixture and reduce until almost dry. Whip in 4 cups of butter (do not allow the butter to break), whipping constantly until the butter is melted. Strain the sauce and then add the mustard and all but ½ tsp of the chives.

To prepare the snapper: Squeeze the juice of the lime and one of the lemons over the snapper. Dredge the fish in seasoned flour. Sauté the snapper in two TBSP of butter until tender and golden.

In a separate pan, sauté ½ tsp of shallots and ½ tsp of fresh chopped chives in two TBSP of butter. Add the crabmeat. Simmer a few minutes, until hot. Spoon the crabmeat over the snapper. Serve the sauce hot over the top.

—Hans Schadler
The Williamsburg Inn
Williamsburg

Lobster and Shrimp Piccata

serves six

12 eggs	2 lemons (juiced)
4 egg yolks	2 large shallots (minced)
2½ cups flour, divided	2 tsp parsley (fresh chopped)
2 cups Parmesan cheese	2 TBSP small capers
2 TBSP basil	2 tomatos (peeled, seeded,
2 TBSP oregano	and chopped)
2 TBSP thyme	½ cup white wine
Paprika to taste	6 lobster tails (split)
Salt and pepper to taste	12 large shrimp
1 cup butter (room temperature)	

To prepare the batter: Combine the eggs, the egg yolks, ½ cup of the flour, the Parmesan cheese, the basil, the oregano, the thyme, paprika, salt, and pepper. Mix the batter well.

To prepare the sauce: Melt the cup of softened butter in a saucepot. Add the lemon juice, the shallots, the parsley, the capers, and the tomatoes. When the butter is almost brown, add the wine and reduce the sauce.

To prepare the piccata: Dredge the lobster tails and the shrimp in the seasoned flour and then dip them in the batter. Sauté the seafood in butter until golden brown. Remove and drain. Gently ladle the shrimp and lobster with sauce.

—Hans Schadler
The Williamsburg Inn
Williamsburg

Braised Mussels, Cherrystone Clams, Sea Scallops and Tomatoes on Saffron and Black Pepper Fettuccine

serves eight

Saffron pasta
1 tsp saffron
1 TBSP water
1¾ to 2 cups flour
2 eggs
1 TBSP olive oil

Black pepper pasta
1¾ to 2 cups flour
2 eggs
1 TBSP olive oil
1 TBSP cracked black pepper
1 to 2 tsp water

3 to 4 TBSP cornmeal
1 lb. tomatoes
24 fresh mussels
24 fresh cherrystone clams
1½ cups mild fish stock *or* water
1 lb. fresh sea scallops
2 shallots (minced)
¼ cup white wine
Salt and pepper to taste
Boiling water

To prepare the pastas: Dissolve the saffron in the water. Put the flour for each pasta in a separate bowl and make a well in the center of each. In each well put the other ingredients for the pastas. First using a fork and then clean dry hands, work the doughs together. Knead the separate doughs well using the other ¼ cup of flour as necessary. Cut the pasta into fettuccine, toss with cornmeal, and refrigerate.

Core the tomatoes and plunge them into boiling, salted water for 30 to 40 seconds and then into ice water. Remove the skins, cut the tomatoes in half horizontally and squeeze out the seeds. Chop the tomatoes into ½-inch cubes.

To prepare the seafood: Clean the mussels and remove the beards. Scrub the clams. In a large covered pot, steam the mussels and the clams in the stock until just open. Remove the mussels and the clams and cool briefly. Strain the stock and reserve warm. Shuck the shellfish discarding the shells. Clean the sea scallops, slicing the largest in half. In a large pan cook the minced shallots in ¼ cup of white wine for 2 minutes. Add the mussels, the clams, the scallops, and the tomatoes. Pour in approximately one cup of the stock. Season to taste with salt and pepper. Meanwhile, shake the excess cornmeal from the pasta. Cook the pasta in boiling salted water for about 1 minute or until tender. Drain the pasta and toss with butter. Divide the pasta equally amongst the hot plates and spoon the seafood and tomatoes over each. Serve immediately.

—Philip Delaplane
The Trellis, Williamsburg

Poached Fillet of Salmon with Cucumber Julienne and Caviar

serves eight

Poaching liquid
Water to cover
½ cup white wine
1 lemon (juiced)
1 tsp salt

8 6-ounce salmon fillets (skinless)
2 TBSP butter

4 shallots (peeled, fine mince)
2 med. cucumbers (peeled, split
   lengthwise, seeded, and julienned)
1 cup heavy cream
2 TBSP parsley (fresh chopped)
Salt and pepper to taste
8 tsp golden caviar

To poach the salmon: Bring the poaching liquid to a boil. Reduce heat until the liquid is barely moving. Add the salmon to the liquid. Cook the salmon for 7 to 10 minutes or until the flesh is just firm to the touch.

To prepare the sauce: In a sauté pan, melt the butter. Add the shallots. Add the julienne of cucumber. Sauté lightly, being careful not to burn the cucumbers. Add the cream and reduce until the cream has reached a "coating" consistency. Stir in the chopped parsley. Season the cucumbers to taste with the salt and pepper.

Remove the salmon from the poaching liquid. Arrange the salmon on a platter. Spoon the sauce over the top. Garnish with the golden caviar.

—Rhys Lewis
The Williamsburg Inn
Williamsburg

Broiled Grouper with Tomatoes, Mushrooms and Scallions

serves eight

Marinade
¼ cup olive oil
4 med. garlic cloves (minced)
Salt to taste
Fresh ground pepper to taste
Dash paprika

8 5- to 6-ounce grouper fillets
   (skinless)
6 TBSP butter

2 shallots (peeled and minced)
8 scallions (trimmed, washed,
   sliced on a bias)
8 to 10 field mushrooms
   (washed and sliced)
4 tomatoes (peeled, seeded,
   and diced)
Dill and parsley (fresh
   chopped for garnish)

To prepare the grouper: To prepare the marinade, combine the oil, and the spices. *Marinate the fish one day in advance.* Remove the grouper from the marinade. Shake off the excess oil. Broil on a hot grill for 5 to 8 minutes, depending on the thickness, or until the flesh just becomes opaque. *Do not overcook!*

For service: In a sauté pan, melt the butter. Add the shallots, the scallions, and the mushrooms. Sauté lightly, about 2 minutes. Add the chopped tomatoes, the dill, and the parsley. Sauté. Season to taste with salt and pepper. Spoon the tomato mixture over the fish, serve.

—Rhys Lewis
The Williamsburg Inn
Williamsburg

Matelote Pecheur

serves six

1 onion	1 tsp thyme
1 carrot	1½ TBSP salt
1 stalk celery	1 tsp pepper
6 to 8 fresh mushrooms	1 tsp nutmeg
2 garlic cloves	1½ cups white wine
1 lb. rockfish fillets	2 cups fish stock (see index)
1 lb. sea trout fillets	2 TBSP butter
1 lb. bluefish	2 TBSP flour
1 lb. perch fillets	3 egg yolks
3 TBSP olive oil	¼ cup heavy cream
2 bay leaves	

To prepare the stew: Slice the onion, the carrot, the celery, and the mushrooms. Crush the garlic. Clean the fish. Wash and dry them well with a towel. Cut the fishes into two-inch square pieces. In a stewing pot, put the olive oil, the onion, the celery, the carrot, the bay leaves, the thyme, the salt, the pepper, the nutmeg and the rockfish. Sauté for 2 minutes. Add the wine and the fish stock. Put the pan on low heat and cook for 3 minutes more. Add the trout and the bluefish. Cook 4 minutes more. Add the perch and simmer the mixture for 8 minutes. Separate the fish from the stock, placing the pieces in a deep serving dish or tureen. Strain the stock and reserve for the sauce.

To prepare the sauce: In another pan melt the butter. Remove the pan from the heat and add the flour and the egg yolks, beating after each addition. Slowly add the strained fish stock, stirring well. Add the cream and stir vigorously to mix all well. Add the mushrooms and stir constantly for about 4 minutes. *Do not heat any longer*, as the mushrooms will get tough.

For service: Pour the sauce over the fish. Serve with boiled potatoes or cooked white noodles tossed with butter and pepper. A Riesling or a California Chenin Blanc would be excellent wine choices.

—Paul Elbling
La Petite France
Richmond

FOWL AND GAME

Of wild Fowl, and hunted Game.

As in Summer, the Rivers and Creeks are filled with Fish, so in Winter they are in many Places cover'd with Fowl. There are such a Multitude of Swans, Geese, Brants, Sheldrakes, Ducks of several Sorts, Mallard, Teal, Blewings, and many other Kinds of Water-Fowl, that the Plenty of them is incridible...

The Shores, Marshy Grounds, Swamps, and Savanna's, are also stor'd with the like Plenty of other Game, of all Sorts, as Cranes, Curlews, Herons, Snipes, Woodcocks, Saurers, Ox-eyes, Plover, Larks, and many other good Birds for the Table that they have not yet found a Name for. Not to mention Beavers, Otters, Musk-Rats, Minxes, and an infinite Number of other wild Creatures.

Altho' the Inner Lands want these Benefits (which, however, no Pond or Slash is without,) yet even they, have the Advantage of Wild Turkeys, of an incredible Bigness, Phaesants, Partridges, Pigeons, and an infinity of small Birds, as well as Deer, Hairs, Foxes, Raccoons, Squirrels, Possums. And upon the Frontier Plantations, they meet with Bears, Panthers, Wild-Cats, Elks, Buffaloes, and Wild Hogs, which yield Pleasure, as well as Profit to the Sports-man.

—Robert Beverly
The History and Present State of Virginia, 1705

Marinated Game Hens with Scallions, Bacon and Pecans

serves eight

Marinade
1½ cups soy sauce
1½ cups peanut oil
1 TBSP ground black pepper

4 game hens
½ lb. bacon (smoked, slab *or* sliced)
3 bunches scallions
½ lb. pecans halves
3 TBSP butter
Salt and pepper to taste

To prepare the game hens: Combine the soy sauce, the peanut oil, and the black pepper. Split the birds in half and prick the skin with a fork. Place them in marination for ½ hour. Cut the bacon into small cubes. Fry the bacon until crisp and drain well. Trim the scallions and slice thinly. Toast the pecans in a 350 degrees F. oven for 5 minutes. Grill the game hens for 35 to 40 minutes, basting them with the marinade until done. Sauté the scallions and the bacon in butter. Season to taste with salt and pepper. Spoon the garnish evenly over the finished hens. Sprinkle each half bird with toasted pecans and serve.

—Philip Delaplane
The Trellis
Williamsburg

Grilled Chicken Breasts with
Artichokes, Roasted Garlic and Rosemary

serves eight

6 fresh artichokes
2 small bulbs garlic
8 8-ounce chicken breasts
   (boneless and skinless)

Salt and pepper to taste
2 TBSP butter
1 large sprig fresh rosemary *or*
   1½ TBSP dried

To prepare the chicken: Prepare the charcoal or wood grill. Trim the artichokes of the outer leaves and remove the chokes. Place the chokes in boiling, salted water and cook for 10 to 12 minutes. Remove the artichokes and chill. Cut the cool chokes into strips. Break the garlic into cloves and roast in a 375 degrees F. oven for 8 to 10 minutes. Remove and gently peel the cloves when cool. Pound the chicken and season with salt and pepper. Grill the chicken for 6 to 8 minutes until done. While the chicken is grilling, sauté the artichoke and the roasted garlic in the butter. Add the snipped rosemary and serve over each chicken breast.

—Philip Delaplane
The Trellis
Williamsburg

Duckling with Sausage Stuffing

serves four

½ lb. bulk pork sausage
4 cups dry bread cubes
1 cup apple (peeled, chopped)
1 cup celery (chopped)
½ cup onion (chopped)
¼ cup parsley (snipped)

½ tsp thyme (dried and crushed)
½ tsp marjoram (dried and crushed)
½ tsp salt
Pepper to taste
4 TBSP water, divided
1 4- to 5-lb. duckling (ready to cook)

To prepare the stuffing: Preheat oven to 375 degrees F. In a skillet, cook the sausage until lightly browned and then drain well. In a large bowl, stir together the cooked sausage, the bread cubes, the apple, the celery, the onion, the parsley, the thyme, the marjoram, the salt, and pepper. Toss the sausage mixture with two TBSP water.

To prepare the duckling: Fill the cavity of the duckling with the stuffing. Reserve any remaining stuffing. Place the bird, breast-side up, on a rack in a shallow roasting pan. Tie the legs together; tie the legs to the tail. Twist the wing tips under the back. Prick the skin all over with a fork. Roast the duckling, uncovered, until tender, about 1½ to 2 hours. Drain off the excess fat as necessary. Place any reserved stuffing in a 1-quart casserole and sprinkle with the remaining two TBSP of water. Cover the stuffing and bake during the last 30 minutes of the duck's cooking time. Serve the stuffing with the duckling.

—Art Cook
The Westwood Racquet Club
Richmond

Gefullte Gans

serves six to eight

1 10- to 12-lb. goose	1 tsp salt
4 TBSP butter	½ tsp pepper
¼ cup onion (chopped)	2 eggs (beaten)
¼ cup celery (chopped)	¼ tsp marjoram leaves
1 whole orange	½ cup chicken stock
2 whole apples	3½ cups soft bread crumbs
2 TBSP Grand Marnier liqueur	(about 5 slices bread)

To prepare the goose: Preheat oven to 325 degrees F. Wash the goose. Rub the inside and outside with salt. In a sauté pan, melt the butter. Sauté the onion and the celery until tender. Remove the vegetables from the heat and allow them to cool. Wash the orange and the apples. Core the apples. Chop both the orange and the apples but not too fine. Add the apples, the Grand Marnier, the salt, the pepper, the beaten eggs, the marjoram, the cooked vegetables, and the chicken broth to the bread crumbs. Fold all together thoroughly. Fill the body and neck cavities of the goose with the stuffing and close with a skewer. Place the goose breast-side down on a rack in a roasting pan. Roast the goose uncovered for 3 hours. Remove the fat from the pan as it accumulates. Turn the goose breast-side up. Roast 1 to 2 hours or longer or until the goose tests done. To test for doneness, twist the leg bone. If the leg bone turns easily the goose is tender and done.

Serve the goose with red cabbage and potato pancakes or dumplings and an orange sauce if desired.

—Manfred E. Roehr
Chowning's Tavern
Williamsburg

Rabbit Fricassee

serves four

¼ cup flour
½ tsp salt
⅛ tsp pepper
1 2- to 2½-lb rabbit
(cut into frying pieces)
1 TBSP butter
1 cup water
2 sprigs parsley
¼ tsp marjoram (dried and crushed)

¼ tsp oregano (dried and crushed)
⅛ tsp allspice (ground)
⅛ tsp cloves (ground)
1 tsp lemon juice

Sauce:
2 TBSP cold water
1 TBSP flour

To prepare the rabbit: Mix together ¼ cup flour, the salt, and the pepper. Coat the rabbit pieces with the flour mixture. In a skillet, brown the rabbit very slowly in butter. Reduce the heat and add one cup of water, the parsley, the marjoram, the oregano, the allspice, and the cloves. Cook the rabbit, covered, until tender, about 1 hour. Remove the rabbit to a warm platter. Discard the parsley. Measure the pan juices, skimming off the fat. Add enough water to make one cup of liquid. Return the liquid to the skillet. Blend the two TBSP of cold water with the one TBSP flour and stir this mixture into the cooking liquid. Cook, stirring, until the gravy is thick and bubbly. Cook 2 more minutes. Season the gravy to taste with salt and pepper. Serve the gravy on the side over rice.

—Art Cook
The Westwood Racquet Club
Richmond

Chicken à la Art Supreme

serves six

6 8-ounce chicken breasts
(fresh, boneless)
6 2-ounce slices Smithfield ham
1 lb. crabmeat
Salt, pepper, and paprika to taste

½ cup (1 stick) butter (melted)
5 tsp flour
2 cups milk (hot)
4 ounces (½ cup) sherry

To prepare the chicken: Preheat oven to 425 degrees F. Pound the chicken breast. Lay a slice of ham and ⅙ of the crabmeat on each piece of chicken and roll. Place the breasts on a baking sheet. Season with salt and pepper to taste. Sprinkle with paprika and lace with butter. Bake for 35 to 40 minutes. Allow 10 minutes before the chicken is done to prepare the sauce.

To prepare the sauce: Into a saucepan over medium heat, pour the drippings from the chicken. Add the flour and stir until the flour is cooked. Add the hot milk, stir until smooth and simmer. Add the sherry and continue to simmer. Season to taste with salt and pepper. Serve with rice.

—Art Cook
The Westwood Racquet Club
Richmond

Grilled Marinated Breast of Chicken with Scallions, Radishes and Fresh Lime

serves eight

8 8-ounce chicken breasts
(fresh boneless)
Lemon juice and salt as needed

Marinade
1 TBSP coriander (whole)
1 TBSP cumin (whole)
4 ounces ginger (grated)
1 TBSP garlic (crushed)
1 tsp cayenne pepper
1 qt. unflavored yogurt

Garnish
Radishes (julienne)
16 scallions (trimmed and washed)
8 limes (quartered)

To prepare the chicken: Sprinkle a light amount of salt and lemon juice over the chicken breasts. Allow the chicken to stand at room temperature for 30 minutes.

To prepare the marinade: Toast the coriander and the cumin on a sheet pan in a 350 degrees F. oven for 5 minutes. Allow the spices to cool; then crush them in a blender or with a mortar and pestle. Combine the coriander and the cumin with the other ingredients for the marinade. Dip the chicken into the yogurt marinade. Refrigerate the marinated chicken for 24 hours.

For service: Julienne the radishes by hand or in a food processor. Grill the chicken breast over a medium hot charcoal and wood fire. Place the chicken on a plate covered with the julienne of radish. Finish the garnish with scallions and limes. Serve immediately.

—Marcel Desaulniers
The Trellis
Williamsburg

80

Chicken with Sausage and Almonds

serves eight

8 8-ounce chicken breasts
  (boneless and skinless)
1½ lbs. bread crumbs (fresh)
1½ lbs. mild sausage
2 ounces blanched almonds
½ lb. Muenster cheese (grated)

1 lb. flour (seasoned)
Salt and pepper to taste
3 eggs
2 pints half and half
Butter or vegetable oil as needed

To prepare the chicken: Take the chicken breasts, without the tenders, and pound with a mallet. Refrigerate. Preheat the oven to 325 degrees F. Prepare the bread crumbs by drying the bread on a sheet pan in the oven for about 10 to 15 minutes. Make crumbs with a grater or a food processor. Brown the sausage, drain the grease, and cool. Combine the almonds and the cheese with the sausage. Put a heaping tablespoon of the sausage mixture on half of each breast and fold the chicken over to form a pocket. Dredge each chicken breast in seasoned flour, coating each side well. Combine the eggs and the half and half to prepare the egg wash. Dip each breast into the egg wash and then into the fresh dry bread crumbs. Be very careful that the crumbs cover all sides of the chicken. In a hot sauté pan, brown the chicken in the butter or oil. Put the chicken breasts on a sheet pan and bake for 25 minutes.

Serve the chicken with a beurre blanc or white wine sauce.

—George W. Clarke III
Country Club of Virginia
Richmond

Oct. 3

One of the Indians shot a wild goose
that was very lousy which nevertheless was
good meat and proved those contemptible
tasters to be no bad tasters.

—William Byrd, 1733

Chicken with Bacon, Onions and Fresh Herbs

serves four

12 chicken thighs *or*
  8 leg and thigh portions
½ cup lemon juice
Salt and fresh ground black
  pepper to taste
4 slices bacon (½-inch pieces) *or*
  if possible, 2 ½-inch strips slab
  bacon (cubed)
½ cup flour (seasoned)

4 small or 2 large onions (sliced)
2 cups dry white wine
2 garlic cloves (whole, peeled)
4 TBSP butter
2 TBSP basil (fresh, chopped)
½ tsp rosemary (fresh *or*
  dried, crushed)
1 tsp thyme (fresh, chopped)

To prepare the chicken: Marinate the chicken with lemon juice, salt, and pepper. Fry the bacon in a cast iron skillet. Preheat oven to 375 degrees F. Remove the bacon from the pan, reserving the fat. Dredge the chicken lightly in the seasoned flour. Fry the chicken in the reserved fat until golden brown on both sides. Remove the chicken from the skillet and hold. Sauté the onions, seasoning them to taste. Add the white wine and the garlic to the pan. Return the chicken and the bacon to the skillet. Top the chicken with bits of butter and the fresh herbs. As soon as the liquid boils, cover the skillet tightly with aluminum foil. Bake until just done and still juicy, about 25 minutes. Serve the chicken and the liquid with rice pilaf.

Note: This recipe is good for almost any game bird and rabbit, as well.

—Jonathan A. Zearfoss
The Trellis
Williamsburg

Blackened Mustard Chicken

serves four

1 lb. chicken breast (fresh, boneless)
¼ cup lemon juice
4 TBSP Dijon-style mustard
Salt and pepper to taste
1 garlic clove (minced)

2 TBSP vegetable oil *or*
  clarified butter
2 tsp basil (dried)
1 tsp thyme (dried)

To prepare the chicken: Twenty-four hours in advance, cut the chicken breast into two-by-½-inch strips and marinate them in lemon juice, mustard, salt, and pepper and garlic. About 5 minutes before service bring two TBSP of vegetable oil or clarified butter to very high temperature in a sauté pan. Add the basil and the thyme and after about ten or fifteen seconds add the chicken and all of the marinade. If the pan is hot enough, the chicken should blacken very quickly and the marinade should dissipate within a few seconds. Sauté the chicken for about 2 minutes, making sure that all the sides have been seared.

Serve the chicken with Peppered Black-eyed Peas and Herbed Rice. (see index).

—George Fransisco, apprentice
The Trellis
Williamsburg

Chicken Tarragon

serves eight

Dressing
½ cup cider vinegar
½ TBSP salt
½ tsp dry mustard
½ TBSP sugar
¼ tsp white pepper
1½ cups vegetable oil
⅛ tsp basil leaves
½ tsp parsley (fresh chopped)
1 small garlic clove (minced)
1 TBSP tarragon leaves

4 lb. chicken (cooked, large dice)
2½ ounces raisins
1 TBSP sesame seeds
1 bunch scallions (½-inch pieces)
1 carrot (sliced, cooked)
4 ounces water chestnuts
½ lb. snow peas (cooked
  al dente, cooled)
6 ounces mandarin orange segments
2 leaves red cabbage (julienned)
½ lb. noodles (fresh if possible,
  cooked and cooled)

To prepare the dressing: Mix all ingredients well. Refrigerate.

To prepare the chilled entree: Mix all of the ingredients with the dressing and refrigerate for 2 to 4 hours. Serve on bibb lettuce or another kind of lettuce greens. Garnish with fresh vegetable flowers if desired.

—Richard J. Nelson
Richmond

Chicken Croquettes

serves four

Sauce
4 TBSP butter
4 TBSP flour
1½ cups chicken stock
½ cup heavy cream
Curry powder to taste
Salt and pepper to taste

2 cups chicken (cooked, chopped)
½ tsp salt
¼ tsp celery salt
Cayenne pepper to taste
1 tsp lemon juice
¼ tsp onion juice
1 tsp parsley (fresh chopped)
½ cup bread crumbs
2 eggs (beaten)

To prepare the sauce: Melt the butter in a small heavy saucepan. Stir in the flour. Blend well, cooking slowly over low heat. Slowly stir in the chicken stock and the cream. Stirring constantly, bring the mixture slowly to a boil and cook for about 2 minutes or until the sauce has thickened. Season the sauce to taste with the curry powder and the salt and pepper. Cool one cup of the sauce and hold the remaining one cup warm (covered).

To prepare the croquettes: Mix together the chicken, the salt, the celery salt, the lemon juice, the onion juice, the parsley, and enough of the cooled sauce to keep the mixture soft but stiff enough to hold its shape. Chill the mixture; then shape into eight croquettes. Heat vegetable oil to 375 to 385 degrees F. Dip the croquettes into the beaten eggs, roll them in bread crumbs, and then fry them for 2 to 4 minutes. Serve the croquettes with the hot cream sauce.

—Eleanor Thompson, apprentice
The Trellis
Williamsburg

Oct. 15

*After our bounteous landlady had
cherished us with roast beef and chicken pie,
we thankfully took our leave.*

—William Byrd 1733

Chicken Legs Stuffed with Duck Livers and Mushrooms

serves four

4 med. chicken legs
3 TBSP butter
½ lb. duck livers
8 fresh mushrooms (chopped)
1 green onion (chopped)
2 TBSP walnuts (chopped)
1 tsp garlic (minced)
Salt and white pepper to taste

4 TBSP Worcestershire sauce
1 cup dry red wine
4 TBSP margarine
½ tsp paprika
4 leaves romaine lettuce
1 red pepper (sliced)
1 orange (half moon slices)
4 TBSP raisins

To prepare the chicken: Preheat oven to 350 degrees F. Cut chicken legs along the bone on the inner side. Remove the bones. Spread the leg with a kitchen hammer. In a sauté pan, melt the butter. Add the duck livers, the mushrooms, the onions, the walnuts, and the garlic. Season the liver mixture to taste with the salt and pepper. Sauté the stuffing until the blood from the livers is gone. Equally distribute the stuffing amongst the chicken legs. With a needle and thread sew the legs back together. Place the chicken legs, thread-side down, in a baking pan. Add the Worcestershire, the wine, and the magarine. Bake the legs for 40 to 50 minutes, adding more wine as needed.

For service: Remove the legs from the oven and place on individual plates on the romaine leaves. Place the slices of red pepper on top of the chicken with the orange slices to the side. Sprinkle with raisins.

—Gideon Hirteinstein
Guest Services, Inc.
Washington, D.C.

MEATS

Oct. 5

*We pursued our journey . . . and . . . had
the fortune to knock down a young buffalo
of two years old. Providence threw this vast
animal in our way very seasonably just as
our provisions began to fail us. And it was
the more welcome, too, because it was a
change of diet, which of all varieties, next to
that of bedfellows, is the most agreeable. We
had lived upon venison and bear until our
stomachs loathed them almost as much as
the Hebrews of old did their quails.*
*Our butchers were so unhandy at their
business that we grew very lank before we
could get our dinner. But when it came we
found it equal in goodness to the best beef.
They made it the longer because they kept
sucking the water out of the guts, in
imitation of the Catawba Indians, upon the
belief that it is a great cordial, and will
make them drunk, or at least gay.*

*—*William Byrd
A Journey to the Land of Eden, Anno 1733

> *Oct. 6*
>
> *We made our supper on the tongue and udder of the buffalo, which were so good that a cardinal legate might have made a comfortable meal upon them during a carnival. Nor was that all, but we had still a rarer morsel, the bunch rising up between the shoulder of this animal which is very tender and very fat.*
>
> —William Byrd
> *A Journey to the Land of Eden,* Anno 1733

Entrecote Mirabeau

serves four

4 sirloins
8 black olives
Butter to taste
8 anchovies
1 tsp tarragon

To prepare the steaks: Pit the olives and chop fine. Sauté the sirloins in butter as desired. Remove the sirloins from the pan and place them in serving dishes. In the same pan, add a bit more butter, the anchovies, the olives, and the tarragon. Sauté these ingredients in the butter until well mixed. Pour an equal amount over each sirloin and serve.

—Paul Elbling
La Petite France
Richmond

Medallions of Beef and Sautéed
Shiitake Mushrooms with Red Wine Sauce

serves four

6 TBSP butter *or* margarine,
   divided
4 small shallots (minced)
1 garlic clove (minced)
½ cup Worcestershire sauce
½ cup red wine (Bordeaux)

¼ lb. mushrooms (fresh, sliced
   Shiitake, if possible)
1½ lbs. beef tenderloin (medallions)
Cognac as needed
1 tsp flour

To make the sauce: In a sauté pan, melt two TBSP of the butter. Sauté the shallots; then add the garlic. After 2 minutes, add the Worcestershire and the wine. Simmer until the sauce is reduced by one third. Add the mushrooms.

To prepare the beef: In a separate pan, melt the remaining butter and, when hot, sauté the beef to the desired degree of doneness. Flame the beef with cognac. Remove the beef. Add the flour to the pan and stir. Mix the beef drippings into the sauce. Set the medallions on a bed of rice and pour the sauce over.

—Dominador Valeros
Virginia Beach Yacht Club
Virginia Beach

Marinated Beef (Sauerbraten)

serves eight

4 lb. blade pot roast of beef
2 carrots
1 med. onion
1 stalk celery
3 cups red wine
½ cup red wine vinegar
2 bay leaves
1 tsp allspice (ground)
½ cup brown sugar

2 tsp salt
½ tsp ground pepper
8 garlic cloves (minced) *or*
   1 tsp granulated garlic powder
6 to 8 whole cloves
2 cups water
1 TBSP butter
½ lb. mushrooms (sliced)
2 cups heavy cream

To prepare the beef: Put the pot roast in a deep pot or pan. Wash the carrots, the onion, and the celery. Cut the vegetables into ¼-inch pieces with the skin and put them in the pot with the beef. In a separate pot, mix together the wine, the vinegar, the spices, and the water. Bring the mixture to a boil. Cool the marinade and, when cool, pour it over the beef. Put the roast in the refrigerator *for at least 72 hours*, turning the beef twice a day. After 3 days remove the beef from the pot. In a skillet, brown the pot roast on all sides. Return the seared beef to a deep pot. Add the marinade. Bring the liquid to a boil and then reduce to a simmer. Allow the beef to simmer for about 2½ hours or until tender. Remove the beef from the pot and hold. Strain and reserve the marinade.

To make the sauce: In a small heavy saucepot, melt the butter. Sauté the mushrooms, seasoning lightly to taste with salt and pepper. Add the cream. Simmer the mixture until the cream is reduced in volume by one third to one half. Pour 2 cups of the strained marinade into the cream mixture. Mix together and bring to a boil. Simmer the mixture for about 10 minutes for a good sweet and sour tasting sauce. Slice the beef thinly and serve with the sauce. Serve noodles, potato pancakes, or potato dumplings as accompaniment.

—Manfred E. Roehr
Chowning's Tavern
Williamsburg

Swiss Meat Pie

serves four

1 lb. pie *or* puff pastry dough	2 TBSP flour
1 large onion (finely chopped)	1 cup red wine
4 strips bacon (cubed)	Salt and pepper to taste
¾ lb. beef (minced)	1 egg
¾ lb. pork (minced)	

To prepare the pie: Preheat oven to 400 degrees F. Roll out ⅔ of the pie dough and line a pie pan. Brown the onion and the bacon cubes in hot fat. Add the beef and the pork and brown, also. Dredge with the flour and quench with the wine. Season the meat to taste with the salt and pepper and simmer for a few minutes. Spread the stuffing evenly over the bottom of the pie. Roll out the remaining third of the dough to form the covering. Spread the egg over the pie rim and cover with the remaining dough. Spread again with egg and press the edges together. Trim the rim and puncture the top with a fork. Bake the pie for approximately 50 minutes.

—Otto Bernet
Chef Otto's Bakery
Richmond

Chili

serves six

1¼ lbs. ground beef
2 cups onion (diced)
1 6-ounce can tomato paste
1 14½-ounce can whole tomatoes
  (with juice)
2½ TBSP chili powder
2½ tsp cumin
1½ tsp salt
1¼ cup water *or* beef stock
⅓ tsp garlic powder *or*
  3 garlic cloves (minced)

1 small bay leaf
1 tsp oregano
¼ tsp cayenne pepper
1 15 ounce-can kidney beans

Garnish
1½ cups Cheddar cheese (grated)
¾ cup onion (coarsely chopped)
6 TBSP sour cream

To prepare the chili: Sauté the meat and the onions over medium heat until the meat loses its pink color. Add all of the remaining ingredients, except the beans. Simmer, stirring occasionally for 1 hour. Add the beans and simmer the mixture for 15 minutes longer. (The chili will hold, refrigerated, for four days at this point; the flavors will mellow and improve with time).

For service: Heat the chili slowly to a simmer. Continue to simmer for 20 minutes, until thoroughly heated, stirring occasionally. Serve the chili in heated crocks or bowls. Top each serving with grated Cheddar cheese, chopped onion and sour cream.

—Mark Kimmel
The Tobacco Company
Richmond

Grilled Lamb Chops with Jalapeño-Mint Butter

serves four

Butter
¼ lb. unsalted butter
  (room temperature)
1 shallot (minced)
1 jalapeño (minced, more if desired)
5 mint leaves (finely chopped)
Salt and white pepper to taste

4 6-ounce lamb chops
¼ cup olive oil
Salt to taste
Black pepper to taste

To prepare the butter: Mix all of the ingredients for the butter thoroughly. Place the compound butter on waxed paper and roll into a cylinder about the same diameter as a quarter. Return the butter to the refrigerator until firm. Slice the butter into eight slices.

To prepare the lamb: Combine the oil, the salt, and the black pepper. Dip each chop into the oil mixture. Cook the chops on a prepared grill to the desired doneness, approximately 3 minutes on each side for medium rare. Place two slices of the butter on each chop and serve immediately.

—Mike Gyetvan
The Trellis
Williamsburg

Mesquite Grilled Tenderloin of Pork with Grapefruit and Mint

serves six

6 pork tenderloins
(cleaned of all excess fat)
1 grapefruit (peeled)
¼ cup honey

4 TBSP mint (fresh chopped)
½ lb. unsalted butter
(room temperature)

To prepare the pork: Place each tenderloin on a sheet of foil and cover with another sheet of foil. Pound the tenderloins with a heavy cleaver or saute pan until they are less than ½ inch thick. Squeeze the peeled grapefruit of all juice. Combine the juice with the honey and two TBSP of chopped mint. Place the tenderloins in the juice and honey mixture and allow them to marinate for *2 to 3 hours before cooking.* If desired, the meat can be removed from the marinade, wrapped in film wrap and held under refrigeration for at least two to three days. Chop the squeezed grapefruit into small pieces. Combine the grapefruit with the remaining two TBSP of mint and work into the softened butter. Spoon the butter mixture into small ramekins. Grill the marinated tenderloins over a medium hot fire. (Pork will dry out and get tough if cooked over too hot a fire). For extra flavor, you may baste the pork with honey while it is grilling. Cook the pork to desired doneness. Serve the grilled pork with an individual ramekin of grapefruit and mint butter.

—Marcel Desaulniers
The Trellis
Williamsburg

Pork Chop Filipinaña

serves four

2 garlic cloves (chopped)
3 TBSP soy sauce
3 TBSP pineapple juice
3 TBSP white vinegar *or*
   lemon juice

1 TBSP white wine
Salt and pepper to taste
1 tsp sugar
4 pork loin chops
1 TBSP cornstarch

To prepare the pork: Mix together the garlic, the soy sauce, the pineapple juice, the vinegar or lemon juice, the wine, the salt and pepper, and the sugar. Pour the marinade over the pork chops in a glass bowl. Cover and refrigerate the pork *for several hours or overnight.* Drain off the liquid, reserving the marinade for the sauce. Roast the chops on a broiler or fry them in clarified butter until golden brown.

To make the sauce: Strain the marinade and mix with the cornstarch. Bring the mixture just to a boil to thicken.

For service: Serve the pork chops over steamed rice. Garnish with peeled and sliced fresh apples which have been sautéed in butter and mint leaves. Pour the sauce over the pork chops before serving.

—Dominador Valeros
Virginia Beach Yacht Club
Virginia Beach

Veal Medallions with Fresh Morels

serves four

8 3-ounce veal medallions
   (lightly pounded)
6 TBSP clarified butter
1 tsp shallots (minced)

1 garlic clove (minced)
½ lb. fresh morels
½ cup apple brandy
½ cup heavy cream

To prepare the veal: Sauté the veal medallions until tender over medium heat. Do not allow the butter to brown. Remove the veal from the pan. To the same pan, add the shallots, the garlic, the morels, the brandy, and the cream and reduce in volume by half. Gently ladle the veal with morel cream.

—Hans Schadler
The Williamsburg Inn
Williamsburg

Stuffed Roast Loin of Pork

serves six

3½ to 4 lbs. pork loin
(about 8 ribs)
¼ lb. prunes (pitted)
1½ tsp onion salt
¼ tsp pepper

1 garlic clove (minced) *or*
⅛ tsp granulated garlic
1 small onion (diced)
1 stalk celery (diced)

To prepare the pork: Preheat oven to 325 degrees F. Take a butcher's steel and enter into the center of the pork loin from both sides until a hole is pushed through. Stuff the loin from both sides with the prunes until the hole is filled. Rub the pork loin with the salt, the pepper, and the garlic. Place the pork loin, fat side up, on a rack in a shallow roasting pan. Add the onion and the celery to the pan. Put the roast, uncovered, in the oven for about 2½ hours. Remove the roast from the oven and allow to sit for about 5 minutes before slicing between each bone. This roast looks very nice with a cooked prune in the center of each serving. Use the pan drippings for a brown gravy to go with the roast.

—Manfred E. Roehr
Chowning's Tavern
Williamsburg

Veal Roll Stuffed with Chunk Lobster Meat

serves six

6 4-ounce veal cutlets
½ cup (1 stick) butter
1 scallion (chopped)
1 stalk celery (chopped)
1 small red pepper (chopped)
1 lb. lobster meat (chopped)
5 tsp bread crumbs
1 egg (hard-cooked, shredded)

2 tsp mayonnaise
½ tsp fresh garlic (minced)
½ tsp oregano
Salt and pepper to taste
6 tomato slices (topped with
grated Parmesan cheese)
¼ cup sour cream
2 tsp parsley (fresh chopped)

To prepare the veal: Pound the veal cutlets and place them on a sheet tray. Melt the butter in a large sauté pan. Add the scallion, the celery, and the red bell pepper. Sauté the vegetables for 4 to 5 minutes. Add the lobster meat to the pan and sauté the mixture for another 4 to 5 minutes.

Remove the mixture from the heat and allow to cool somewhat. Add the bread crumbs, egg, the mayonnaise, the garlic and the oregano. Season to taste with salt and pepper. Chill the mixture for 10 to 15 minutes. Preheat oven to 350 degrees F. Divide the stuffing equally amongst the veal cutlets and roll, being sure the stuffing is inside. Place the veal rolls on a sheet pan, cover with butter, and bake for 4 to 5 minutes or until hot through. Cook the veal immediately before serving.

For service: Garnish each plate with a tomato slice. Place two tsp sour cream on top of the veal and sprinkle with parsley.

—Gideon Hirteinstein
Guest Services, Inc.
Washington, D.C.

Veal

serves four

12 artichoke bottoms (poached)	2 TBSP butter (clarified)
Salt to taste	2 TBSP vermouth
Lemon juice to taste	
6 to 8 ounces Boursin cheese	**Garnish**
8 4-ounce veal cutlets (pounded)	1 lemon (eight wedges)
White pepper to taste	4 parsley sprigs
	4 whole shrimp (peeled, deveined)

To prepare the veal: Purée the artichoke bottoms, the salt, the lemon juice, and the Boursin in a blender and reserve. Heat a sauté pan. Season the veal lightly with salt and white pepper. Add the clarified butter to the sauté pan and sauté the veal for 15 seconds on each side. Transfer the scallopini to a warm serving dish. Drain the excess butter from the sauté pan and deglaze the pan with the vermouth. Reduce the liquid by $\frac{1}{8}$. Add the artichoke purée to thicken the sauce. Simmer the sauce and adjust the seasoning to taste with salt and pepper. Ladle the sauce over the veal and garnish the serving dish with the lemon wedges, the parsley, and the shrimp. Serve immediately.

—Dominador Valeros
Virginia Beach Yacht Club
Virginia Beach

Scallopini of Veal
"St. Moritz"

serves six

3 ounces fresh morels *or*
   1½ ounces dried
20 to 24 ounces top round of veal
   (cut into 1- to 1½-ounce scallopini)
6 TBSP flour
⅛ tsp nutmeg
1 tsp salt
½ tsp freshly ground black pepper

1 cup (2 sticks) unsalted
   sweet butter
1½ bottles dry white wine
1 cup cider vinegar
2 TBSP shallots (minced)
½ cup heavy cream
4 whole eggs (beaten)
½ cup butter (1 stick) (clarified)

To prepare the veal: If using dried morels, rehydrate them in a few TBSP of sherry. Flatten the individual veal slices to ⅛ of an inch with the smooth side of a meat mallet or a cleaver. Cover the veal with plastic wrap and hold at room temperature. Mix the flour with the nutmeg, the salt, and the pepper. Cut the butter into ¼-inch slices and refrigerate. In a high-sided saucepan on high heat put the wine, the vinegar and the shallots and reduce in volume by half. Add the coarsely chopped morels to the reduction and continue cooking until the mixture reaches the consistency of syrup. On medium heat, whisk in the chunks of butter two at a time, being careful not to add the butter too fast as to cool the sauce. Also, if the sauce is brought to too rapid a boil it will separate. If this happens, try adding a few drops of ice cold water. If this fails, begin the sauce again. When all of the butter has been added, reduce the heat to low and slowly whisk in the room temperature cream. Remove the sauce from the heat and hold warm (about 90 degrees F.) Dredge the scallopini first in the seasoned flour and then in the egg and drain briefly. Heat just enough clarified butter to coat the bottom of a skillet. Sauté the veal, a few pieces at a time, in the very hot skillet, adding butter as necessary. Turn the veal after 20 or 30 seconds when slightly browned. Sauté another 20 seconds, remove the veal, and pat dry with a paper towel. Serve three scallopini per portion and top with two TBSP of the sauce. Serve the veal with fresh whole wheat pasta or rissole potatoes.

—Robert B. Ramsey
Richmond

Escallopini of Veal with Lemon and Parmesan

serves eight

8 5-ounce veal cutlets
Salt and white pepper to taste
Flour (seasoned with sage)
2 TBSP vegetable oil *or*
   clarified butter

8 TBSP butter
4 shallots (minced)
1 lemon
4 TBSP veal *jus or* brown sauce
2 ounces Parmesan (fresh grated)

To prepare the veal: Lightly pound the veal cutlets between sheets of plastic with the flat side of a meat pounder. Season the veal with salt and pepper. Dredge the cutlets in the flour seasoned with sage. Shake off the excess flour. Put the oil in a sauté pan. When the oil is hot, sauté the veal cutlets briefly, about 30 seconds on each side. Remove the veal to a serving platter. Pour off the oil and replace with fresh butter. Add the shallots, being careful not to let them burn. Squeeze the lemon into the pan. Add the veal jus (thickened stock), whipping with a wire whisk until smooth. Add the grated Parmesan, whipping until smooth. Pour the sauce immediately over the veal and serve. *This dish must be prepared at the last minute.* Serve with a fresh pasta.

—Rhys Lewis
The Williamsburg Inn
Williamsburg

MEATLESS DISHES

> *Bad commentators spoil the best of books,*
> *So God sends meat, (they say,) the devil*
> *cooks.*
> *The poor man must walk to get meat for*
> *his stomach, the rich man to get stomach for*
> *his meat.*
>
> —Benjamin Franklin
> *Poor Richard's Almanac, 1733-58*

Fondue

serves one

1 garlic clove
½ cup dry white wine
1 cup (6 ounces) Switzerland
   Swiss cheese

½ tsp cornstarch
1 TBSP Kirsch
Nutmeg and pepper to taste
French bread (crusty)

To prepare the fondue: Rub the inside of your skillet or chafing dish with the garlic. Heat the wine. Gradually add the cheese, stirring constantly. Dissolve the cornstarch in the Kirsch. As the cheese mixture begins to cook, stir in the Kirsch. Season with the nutmeg and the pepper. Serve immediately, keeping the fondue hot in the chafing dish or on a small spirit-stove which can be regulated.

To eat the fondue: Each guest spears a small piece of bread with his fondue fork, dips it into the savory fondue, stirs around the pot once or twice, and pops the delicious morsel into his mouth.

A most important fondue rule—he who loses a piece of bread in the pot has to pay for a bottle of wine or the next fondue. Only ladies are free from this venerable law—they forfeit a kiss for every piece of bread they lose.

—Otto Bernet
Chef Otto's Bakery
Richmond

Welsh Rarebit

serves four

4 TBSP butter
1 cup light beer *or* ale
  (room temperature)
2 egg yolks
1 tsp dry mustard

Cayenne pepper to taste
2 tsp Worcestershire sauce
3 cups (½ lb.) aged Cheddar
  (coarsely grated)

To prepare the rarebit: In a double boiler, melt the butter. Beat together the ale, the egg yolks and the seasonings. Add the cheese to the butter a little at a time, stirring constantly. As the cheese melts, add a little of the ale mixture. Continue stirring! When all of the cheese is in and melted and sufficient ale has been added to make a smooth sauce, cook, over low heat for 10 minutes, stirring constantly. *Do not boil!* Keep the mixture hot; if the sauce gets too thick, add more ale. Keep stirring until the mixture appears as smooth as thick cream. Serve immediately over toasted bread of your choice. Top the rarebit with several tomato slices and chopped fresh parsley or basil if available.

—Karen Adkins, apprentice
The Trellis
Williamsburg

Many a meal is lost for want of meat.

—Benjamin Franklin

DESSERTS

Victoria Buttle

. . . 'Coffee? What the devil is this? I thought
the agreement was when you finally
consented to Gavin to buy that horse that he
would neither ask for nor even accept a
spoonful of coffee until he was eighteen years
old:' and his mother not even listening, with
the same hand and in the same manner
half shoving and half popping the cream
pitcher then the sugar bowl into his reach
and already turning back toward the
kitchen, her voice not really hurried and
impatient: just brisk:

'Drink it now. We're already late:' . . . So
he drank the coffee which the soap and
water and hard towelling had unfogged him
enough to know he didn't like and didn't
want but not enough for him to choose what
simple thing to do about it: that is not drink
it: tasting, sipping then adding more sugar
to it until each—coffee and sugar—ceased to
be either and became a sickish quinine sweet
amalgam of the worst of both until his uncle
said,

'Dammit, stop that,' and got up and went
to the kitchen and returned with a saucepan
of heated milk and a soup bowl and dumped
the coffee into the bowl and poured the hot
milk into it and said, 'Go on. Forget about
it. Just drink it.' So he did, from the bowl in
both hands like water from a gourd . . .

—William Faulkner
Intruder in the Dust, 1948

CHOCOLATE

Charlotte Russe Noir

serves four

Chocolate Bavarian Cream
½ ounce plain gelatin
5 egg yolks
4 ounces bittersweet Bavarian
    chocolate
1 ounce unsweetened chocolate

1 pint milk
½ lb. (8 oz.) sugar
½ cup Tia Maria liqueur
1 pint heavy cream (whipped)
Ladyfingers as needed

To prepare the Bavarian cream: Soak the gelatin in cold water. Beat the egg yolks slightly. Melt the chocolate in a double boiler. In a saucepan or double boiler, combine the milk and the sugar and bring the mixture to a boil. Remove the liquid from the heat and pour it slowly over the eggs, stirring well, blending all ingredients rapidly. Add the soaked gelatin and the chocolate. Stir well to completely combine the chocolate and the custard. Add the Tia Maria. When the mixture begins to set and thicken, fold in cream, mixing thoroughly.

To prepare the Charlotte Russe Noir: Line an 8-inch charlotte mold with ladyfingers. Pour the Bavarian cream into the mold. Cool, unmold, and decorate the dessert with an addition ⅓ cup of whipped cream. Pile extra large chocolate shavings high in the center of the charlotte.

—Rolf Herion
Colonial Williamsburg
Williamsburg

101

Chocolate Pot De Crême "Mary"

serves eight

12 eggs yolks
3 TBSP sugar
4¼ cups half and half

4 ounces semi-sweet chocolate
1½ ounces unsweetened chocolate

To prepare the pot de crème: Preheat oven to 325 degrees F. Mix the yolks and the sugar until thick and lemon-colored. Heat the half and half to about 100 degrees F. Melt the chocolate in a double boiler. Combine the half and half with the yolk and sugar mixture. Pour this liquid in a slow and steady stream into the chocolate. It is essential to stir the mixture at all times until the chocolate becomes glossy and smooth. Stir in the half and half mixture until all is combined. After the foam has settled, pour the custard into ovenproof serving dishes. Place the dishes in a cake pan with enough warm water to surround the dishes halfway up the side. Bake for about 30 minutes or until just set. Do not overcook this delicate custard which can be served warm or cold and is excellent with fresh berries.

—Marcel Walter
Colonial Williamsburg
Williamsburg

Brownies

yields twenty

1 cup (2 sticks) butter
8 ounces unsweetened chocolate
7 whole eggs
3 cups sugar

½ tsp vanilla extract
2 cups flour
1 TBSP baking powder
2 cups pecans (chopped)

To prepare the brownies: Preheat oven to 350 degrees F. Melt and combine the butter and the chocolate in a double boiler. Whip the eggs, the sugar, and the vanilla until frothy. Add the chocolate mixture to the egg mixture and blend in the sifted flour, the baking powder, and the pecans. Pour the batter into a 12-by-15-inch pan and bake the brownies for about 35 minutes. Cool and cut the brownies into three-by-three-inch squares.

—Rolf Herion
Colonial Williamsburg
Williamsburg

Black Bottom Cupcakes

yields eighteen to twenty

1 cup cream cheese
1⅓ cup sugar, divided
1 cup chocolate chips
1 egg (unbeaten)
⅛ tsp salt
1 cup sliced almonds
1½ cups flour

¼ cup cocoa
½ tsp salt
1 tsp baking soda
1 cup water
1 TBSP vinegar
⅓ cup vegetable oil
1 tsp vanilla extract

To prepare the cupcakes: Preheat oven to 350 degrees F. In a bowl, mix together the cream cheese, ⅓ cup of sugar, the chocolate chips, the egg, and the ⅛ tsp of salt. Sift together the flour, the cocoa, the ½ tsp of salt, one cup of sugar, and the baking soda. Beat the water, the vinegar, the oil, and the vanilla into the flour mixture. Put paper pastry cups into muffin tins and fill each one third full with the batter. Add two tsp of the chocolate chip mixture on the top of the batter in each cup. Top each with sliced almonds. Bake the cupcakes for 30 to 35 minutes.

—Mitford Sims III
The Tobacco Company
Richmond

Chocolate Pound Cake

serves eight

1½ cups (3 sticks) butter
5 eggs
1 cup milk
3 cups sugar
3 cups flour

½ tsp baking powder
½ tsp salt
½ cup cocoa
1 TBSP vanilla extract
1 cup black walnuts (chopped)

To prepare the cake: Preheat oven to 325 degrees F. Warm the butter, the eggs, and the milk to room temperature. Oil and dust a tube pan. Cream the butter and the sugar until light. Add the eggs one at a time and beat until fluffy. Sift together the flour, the baking powder, the salt, and the cocoa. Add the flour mixture to the butter mixture, one quarter or less at a time, alternating with the milk and the vanilla. Add the nuts. Pour the batter into the tube pan and bake for 1½ hours or until done.

—Mitford Sims III
The Tobacco Company
Richmond

The Trellis Chocolate Mousse Cake

serves eight to ten

Icing
¼ lb. unsweetened chocolate
¼ lb. sweet butter (cubed)
4 egg yolks
½ cup sugar
3 egg whites
1 TBSP powdered cocoa
1 tsp confectioner's sugar

Cake
¼ lb. sweet baking chocolate
¼ lb. butter (cubed)
4 egg yolks
½ cup sugar
3 egg whites

To prepare the mousse cake: Preheat the oven to 325 degrees F. Put the chocolate squares and the butter for the icing in a double boiler and heat slowly until melted. Follow the same procedure with the chocolate and the butter for the cake recipe. In two separate bowls of an electric mixer, combine the egg yolks and the sugar for each recipe. Beat each batch until the mixtures are light and lemon-colored. Add each chocolate mixture to each separate egg mixture, stirring each to blend thoroughly. Beat the egg whites for each recipe until stiff but not brittle. Add half of each batch of egg whites to the respective chocolate mixture and beat. Fold in the remaining egg whites. Butter the sides and bottom of an 8-inch springform pan. Pour all of the sweet chocolate mixture into the pan. Set aside the unsweetened chocolate mixture to use for the icing. Place the springform pan in the oven and bake for approximately 60 minutes. When the cake is done, transfer it to a rack and allow the cake to cool for 15 to 20 minutes. Turn the cake out onto a cake circle or a plate. Allow the cake to stand until thoroughly cooled. Ice the sides and the top of the cake with the icing mixture. Sprinkle the top of the cake with powdered cocoa in a sieve. Add the confectioner's sugar to the sieve and sprinkle over the top of the cake.

—Marcel Desaulniers
The Trellis
Williamsburg

Chocolate and Raspberry Mousse

serves four to six

8 ounces semi-sweet chocolate
(broken into pieces)
1 TBSP butter
4 egg yolks (well-beaten)

2 TBSP raspberry liqueur
2 cups heavy cream
Fresh raspberries as needed

To prepare the mousse: In a double boiler, over low heat, gently melt the chocolate and the butter. Thoroughly beat in the egg yolks and the raspberry liqueur. Set aside. Whip the heavy cream to soft peaks. Transfer the chocolate mixture to a large bowl and carefully fold in the whipped cream. When thoroughly blended, spoon the mixture into individual serving dishes and chill for 2 to 3 hours. Garnish the mousse with fresh raspberries and, if desired, additional whipped cream. Serve immediately.

—Rachel Plotz, apprentice
The Trellis
Williamsburg

White Chocolate Chocolate Chunk Brownies with Pistachio Truffle Filling

serves six to eight

White chocolate brownie
5 ounces white chocolate
5 ounces unsalted sweet butter
4 eggs
1 cup sugar
2 tsp Frangelico
1 cup flour
¼ tsp salt
5 ounces semi-sweet chocolate
(broken into bits)

Truffle filling
4 ounces semi-sweet chocolate
1 ounce (2 TBSP) Frangelico
2 ounces unsalted sweet butter
1 egg yolk
¼ lb. pistachios (shelled, peeled, and ground)

Coating
4 ounces semi-sweet chocolate
1 ounce (2 TBSP) heavy cream

To prepare the brownie: Preheat oven to 350 degrees F. Melt the white chocolate and the butter in a double boiler. Beat together the eggs, the sugar, and the 2 tsp of Frangelico. Add the white chocolate mixture to the egg mixture and stir just to blend. Add the sifted flour and the salt and again stir until just mixed. Fold in the bits of chocolate. Bake the brownie in a round cake pan for about 45 minutes. While the brownies are baking, prepare the truffle filling.

To prepare the truffle filling: Melt the chocolate, with the Frangelico, in a double boiler. Allow the two ounces of butter, cut into bits, to soften. In an electric mixer, beat the egg yolks. Add the chocolate mixture and beat just enough to mix. Add the butter, bit by bit, until all is combined. Fold in the ground pistachios.

To prepare the chocolate coating: In a double boiler gently melt the chocolate with the cream, stirring to combine.

Remove the brownies from the oven and allow to cool on a rack. Split the brownie horizontally. Spread the truffle mixture evenly between the layers of white chocolate brownie. Refrigerate the filled brownie. Coat the cool cake with the chocolate and cream mixture. Refrigerate and allow the coating to harden somewhat. Cut the cake. Serve at room temperature.

—Jonathan A. Zearfoss
The Trellis
Williamsburg

Dec. 19, 1739
I prayed and had hominy. I danced...I ate sausage and eggs and ate too much.
Jan. 20, 1740
I prayed and had coffee. I danced...I ate boiled mutton.
Jan. 23
I prayed and had milk porridge. I danced...dinner—fowl fricassee.
April 11
I read news till dinner and then ate bacon and asparagus.
April 14
I rose about 6 and prepared for my journey to Williamsburg. I prayed and had chocolate.

—William Byrd
Another Secret Diary...

Death by Chocolate

serves eight to twelve

Cocoa meringue

4 egg whites (reserve yolks)
⅛ tsp cream of tartar
⅛ tsp salt
1¼ cups sugar, divided
2 TBSP sifted cocoa
1 TBSP cornstarch

Chocolate brownie

3 ounces sweet chocolate
1½ ounces unsweetened chocolate
4 TBSP unsalted butter
3 eggs
¾ cup sugar
1 tsp vanilla extract
2 TBSP sour cream
½ cup flour (unsifted)
½ tsp baking powder
½ tsp salt

Chocolate ganache

18 ounces sweet chocolate
1½ cups heavy cream
3 TBSP unsalted butter

Mocha mousse

14 ounces sweet chocolate
4 ounces unsweetened chocolate
2 TBSP sifted cocoa
6 TBSP strong, brewed coffee
2 TBSP instant espresso powder
5 egg whites
2 TBSP sugar
2 egg yolks (reserved
    from meringue)
¾ cup heavy cream

Chocolate mousse

12 ounces sweet chocolate
3 cups heavy cream
6 egg whites
¼ cup sugar

Mocha rum sauce

½ cup (1 stick) unsalted butter
1 cup sugar
⅓ cup sifted cocoa
2 TBSP dark rum
1 cup heavy cream
⅛ tsp salt
1 tsp instant espresso powder
1 tsp vanilla extract

To prepare the cocoa meringue: Preheat oven to 300 degrees F. Beat the egg whites, the cream of tartar, and the salt until soft peaks form. Continue beating, gradually adding ½ cup of sugar. Beat the mixture until stiff. Place the remaining sugar, the cocoa, and the cornstarch on top of the egg whites and gently fold together. Using a 9-inch cake pan as a guide, trace a circle on a piece of parchment paper. Turn the paper over and place on a baking sheet. With a pastry bag and a straight tip, fill the circle with meringue, starting in the center and forming a spiral out to the edge. Pin down each corner of the parchment with a dab of meringue. Bake the meringue for 2 hours, or until dry. Check often so that the bottom does not burn. Prepare the chocolate brownie.

To prepare the chocolate brownie: Melt the chocolate and the butter in a double boiler. In an electric mixer, beat the eggs, the sugar, and the vanilla on high until light and doubled in volume. Stir in the chocolate mixture and the sour cream. Sift together the flour, the baking powder, and the salt and gently fold the dry ingredients into the beaten mixture. Grease a 9-inch cake pan. Cut parchment to fit the pan and grease the parchment, also. Scrape the batter into the pan and bake at 300 degrees F. for 15 minutes, or until the center feels set. Be careful not to overbake. Cool the brownie in the pan for 5 minutes. Remove the brownie to a wire rack and refrigerate until firm enough to slice in half.

To prepare the chocolate ganache: Stirring constantly, melt the mixture in a double boiler until smooth. Hold the ganache at room temperature until ready to use.

To prepare the mocha mousse: In a double boiler, melt the chocolate with the cocoa, the coffee, and the espresso powder. While the chocolate is melting, beat the egg whites to soft peaks. Gradually add the sugar and beat until stiff peaks form. Remove the chocolate from the heat and beat in the egg yolks, continuing to beat until the mixture is smooth. Fold half of the egg whites into the chocolate mixture and set aside. Beat the cream until stiff. Place the remaining egg whites on top of the chocolate mixture and the beaten cream on top of the egg whites. Fold the mixture together thoroughly and chill.

To prepare the chocolate mousse: In a clean bowl, over a double boiler, melt the chocolate. Meanwhile, whip the cream in a chilled bowl, until stiff peaks form. Refrigerate the whipped cream. In another bowl, beat the egg whites until soft peaks form. Gradually add the sugar and continue to beat until stiff. Add ¼ of the whipped cream to the melted chocolate and beat vigorously. Quickly add the chocolate to the egg whites and then place the remaining whipped cream on top, folding the mixture together thoroughly. Chill until ready to decorate the cake.

To assemble the Death by Chocolate: Using four to six toothpicks inserted into its sides as guides, slice the brownie horizontally into halves. Place the bottom half in a 9-by-3-inch springform pan. Pour half of the chocolate ganache on top of the brownie and spread evenly. Trim the meringue layer to fit the pan and place it on top of the ganache. Spoon the mocha mousse on top of the meringue, spreading evenly. Place the remaining brownie layer on top of the mocha mousse. Chill the cake in the freezer for 30 minutes. Remove the cake from the freezer and cut around the edges to release the cake from the pan. Carefully pour the remaining ganache over the cake, spreading the ganache evenly on the top and the sides. Chill the cake for 15 minutes to set the ganache. Using a pastry bag and a #5 star tip, cover the top of the cake with the (reserved) chocolate mousse. Chill the cake for one hour.

To prepare the mocha rum sauce: In a saucepan, melt the butter. Add the sugar, the cocoa, the rum, the cream, and the salt. Bring the mixture to a boil. Add the espresso powder, stirring to dissolve. Simmer the mixture for 5 minutes. Remove from the heat and stir in the vanilla. The sauce will stay liquid when cold.

Flood the plates with mocha rum sauce and place a piece of Death by Chocolate in the center.

—Andrew O'Connell
The Trellis
Williamsburg

CAKES AND COOKIES

Cake "Sans Rival"

serves four

8 egg whites
1 cup sugar
2 cups (1 pound) cashews (chopped)

Filling
1 cup sugar
½ cup water
1 tsp. corn syrup
8 egg yolks
5 TBSP butter

To prepare the cake: Preheat oven to 300 degrees F. Beat the egg whites until they are stiff. Gradually add one cup of sugar, beating continuously, until stiff, soft peaks form. Fold in 1½ cups of chopped cashews. Grease and dust lightly with flour four 9-by-14-inch cookie sheets. Pour the mixture onto the sheets and spread thinly. Bake for about 30 minutes or until golden brown. When done, remove from the cookie sheets. Set the cake aside to cool.

To prepare the filling: In a saucepan, bring one cup of sugar, the water, and the corn syrup to a boil without stirring. When thick enough to form a soft ball when dropped into water, remove the syrup from the heat and allow to cool. Beat the egg yolks until thick and lemon-colored. Add the syrup to the egg yolks, little by little, beating well. Cream the butter. Add the syrup mixture to the butter, continuing to cream. Spread the layers with the butter mixture and assemble, in sandwich fashion. Spread the top layer and sides with more of the butter mixture. Sprinkle the top with chopped cashews. Wrap the cake in waxed paper and chill before serving.

—Dominador Valeros
Virginia Beach Yacht Club
Virginia Beach

111

Pecan Whiskey Cake

serves six

3 eggs (separated)	1 lb. pecans
1 cup sugar	12 ounces golden raisins
1 ounce butter (room temperature)	½ tsp baking powder
½ cup light brown sugar	½ tsp nutmeg
1 lb. cake flour	½ cup bourbon whiskey

To prepare the cake: Preheat oven to 250 degrees F. Beat the egg whites to soft peaks and set aside. Beat half of the sugar (½ cup) with the egg yolks and set aside. Cream the butter. Gradually beat the brown sugar and ¼ cup of the granulated sugar into the butter. Add the egg yolk mixture to the butter mixture and beat well. Mix half of the flour (1 cup) with the pecans and the raisins. Sift the rest of the flour together with the baking powder and the nutmeg. Add the sifted mixture to the butter mixture. Add the bourbon whiskey. Stir in the flour, nut, and raisin mixture. Gently fold in the reserved egg whites. Fill a buttered loaf pan with the mixture. Bake the cake for 2 hours or until done.

—Dominador Valeros
Virginia Beach Yacht Club
Virginia Beach

Chilled Strawberry Meringue Cake
(Sacherin aux Fraises, Chantilly)

serves four

Meringue
4 egg whites
1 cup sugar

1 pint fresh strawberries
4 TBSP confectioner's sugar (divided)
1½ pints heavy cream

To prepare the meringue: Butter a sheet pan and dust it with flour. With a pointed instrument, mark three circles, each 6 inches in diameter, in the flour. Preheat the oven to 200 to 250 degrees F. Beat the egg whites, adding the sugar a little at a time, until stiff. Fill a pastry bag, equipped with a half-inch plain tip, with the meringue. Dress a lattice pattern into the three circles. Bake the meringue for about 2 hours, or until dry. Leave the oven door slightly ajar to allow steam to escape.

To prepare the cake: Wash the strawberries and remove the stems. Slice or cut the berries into small pieces. Whip the cream with two TBSP of the confectioner's sugar. Carefully combine the strawberries, two thirds of the whipped cream, and the remaining sugar. Place the strawberry mixture between layers of the meringue. Decorate the top with the remaining whipped cream and some nice strawberries.

—Otto Bernet
Chef Otto's Bakery
Richmond

Colonial Fruitcake

serves eight to ten

1 cup sugar
1 cup (2 sticks) butter
5 eggs
1 tsp orange flavoring
1 tsp lemon flavoring

2 cups flour (sifted)
⅛ tsp baking powder
½ cup pecans or walnuts (chopped)
1 cup glazed mixed fruit (cherries, pineapple, lemon, and orange)

To prepare the fruitcake: Be sure that all ingredients are at room temperature. Preheat oven to 325 degrees F. Grease a loaf pan and dust lightly with flour. Cream the sugar together with the butter. Add the eggs one at a time, beating well after each addition. Add the orange and the lemon flavorings. Sift the flour (reserve 2 TBSP) together with the baking powder. Gradually stir these dry ingredients into the egg mixture. Dredge the nuts and the fruit in the reserved flour. Stir the nuts and fruit into the cake mixture. Spoon the mixture into the prepared loaf pan. Bake the fruitcake for 70 minutes or for 60 minutes if a tube pan is used.

—Rolf Herion
Colonial Williamsburg
Williamsburg

Wholewheat Pound Cake
serves eight

1½ cups honey, divided
1½ cups vegetable oil
¼ tsp salt
6 eggs (separated)
6 TBSP orange rind (grated)

¾ cup orange juice
¼ tsp mace
2 cups wholewheat pastry flour
  (sifted)

To prepare the pound cake: Preheat oven to 300 degrees F. In a large bowl, combine one cup of the honey, all of the oil, and the salt. Beat in the egg yolks, one at a time. Beat the mixture very well. Stir in the orange rind, the orange juice, the mace, and the flour. Whip the egg whites with the remaining honey until stiff. Fold the meringue into the flour mixture. Pour the mixture into an oiled and floured loaf pan or tube pan. Bake the pound cake for about 1 hour, or until the cake springs back gently.

—Mitford Sims III
The Tobacco Company
Richmond

Orange-Nut Pound Cake

serves eight to ten

1 cup sugar
1 cup (2 sticks) butter
5 eggs
1 tsp orange flavoring

2 cups flour (sifted)
⅛ tsp baking powder
½ cup pecans (chopped)

To prepare the pound cake: Preheat oven to 325 degrees F. Be sure that all ingredients are at room temperature. Grease a loaf pan and dust lightly with flour. Cream the sugar and the butter together. Add the eggs one at a time, beating well after each addition. Add the orange flavoring. Sift the flour and the baking powder together, and gradually stir these dry ingredients into the egg mixture. Add the pecans. Spoon the mixture into the prepared loaf pan. Bake the pound cake for 70 minutes if a loaf pan is used *or* 60 minutes for a tube pan.

—Rolf Herion
Colonial Williamsburg
Williamsburg

Honey and Orange Cheesecake

serves eight

1 lb. graham crackers
2 cups sugar, divided
3 TBSP butter
2½ lbs. cream cheese
1 tsp salt

3 TBSP flour
5 whole eggs
4 egg yolks
2 oranges (zested, juiced)
¾ cup honey

To prepare the crust: In a food processor, grind the graham crackers with ¼ cup of the sugar. Add the butter and pulse until the butter is completely incorporated. Press the graham cracker mixture into a buttered springform pan, extending all the way up the sides to the top.

To prepare the cheesecake: Preheat oven to 325 degrees F. In a mixer on low speed, beat the cream cheese, the salt, the flour, and the remaining 1¾ cup of sugar. Increase the speed to medium; add the eggs one at a time, scraping the bowl often. With the speed set on high, beat the mixture until smooth, about two minutes. Add the yolks one at a time, beating on high, until thoroughly incorporated. Add the orange juice and zest and the honey. Stir to mix well. Pour the mixture into the prepared pan and bake for 15 minutes. Reduce the heat to 250 F. and bake for 2 hours or until the center of the cake feels set. Turn the oven off and allow the cake to remain in the oven for one hour. Leave the cake at room temperature for one hour and then chill for two to three hours before serving.

—Andrew O'Connell
The Trellis
Williamsburg

Caramel Pecan Cheesecake

serves ten to twelve

1 cup graham cracker crumbs
¾ cup pecans (ground)
¼ cup sugar
¼ cup butter or margarine (melted)
1½ cups cream cheese
　(room temperature)

¾ cup prepared caramel-flavored
　sauce
3 eggs
2 TBSP milk
½ cup sour cream
Pecan halves as needed

To prepare the crust: In a mixing bowl, combine the graham cracker crumbs, the ground pecans, the sugar, and the butter or margarine. Pat the mixture onto the botton and 1½ inches up the sides of an 8-inch springform pan.

To prepare the cheesecake: Preheat oven to 350 degrees F. In a mixer, on medium speed, beat the cream cheese until fluffy. Gradually beat in ½ cup of the caramel topping. Add the eggs and the milk, beating until just blended. Turn the mixture out into the prepared crust. Bake for 40 to 45 minutes, until the center is set. Cool the cheesecake in the pan for fifteen minutes. Combine the sour cream and the remaining ¼ cup of the caramel topping. Spoon the mixture over the cheesecake. Loosen the sides of the cheesecake from the pan with a spatula. Cool the cake for 30 minutes more and then remove the sides of the springform pan. Chill. Garnish the cake with the pecan halves before serving.

—Paul W. Smith
Colonial Williamsburg
Williamsburg

Pumpkin and Cream Cheese Cake

serves ten

¾ cup flour
1 tsp baking powder
2 tsp ground cinnamon
1 tsp pumpkin pie spice
½ tsp ground nutmeg
½ tsp salt
3 eggs (slightly beaten)
1 cup sugar

⅔ cup canned pumpkin
1 cup walnuts (chopped)

Filling
1 cup confectioner's sugar
1 cup cream cheese
6 TBSP butter
1 tsp vanilla extract

To prepare the cake: Preheat the oven to 375 degrees F. Grease a half-size baking sheet. Line the sheet pan with parchment paper. Grease and flour the paper. Mix the flour, the baking powder, the cinnamon, the pumpkin pie spice, the nutmeg, and the salt together. Blend these dry ingredients well with a wire whip. Beat the eggs and the sugar in a large bowl until thick. Beat in the pumpkin. Stir in the dry ingredients, all at once. Pour the mixture onto the prepared pan and spread evenly with a spatula. Sprinkle with the walnuts. Bake the cake for 15 minutes, or until the center springs back slowly when touched with a fingertip. Loosen the cake around the edges with a knife. Invert the cake onto a clean damp towel which has been dusted with confectioner's sugar. Peel off the parchment. Trim the sides. Roll up the cake and towel together from the long side. Place the cake, seam side down, on a rack and cool.

To prepare the filling: Combine the confectioner's sugar, the cream cheese, the butter, and the vanilla and beat until smooth and fluffy.

To assemble the cake: Unroll the cake. Remove the towel. Spread the cream cheese filling over the cake. Reroll the cake and refrigerate until ready to serve.

—Charlie F. Baker III, apprentice
Sheraton Airport Inn
Richmond

Coconut Macaroons

yields twelve to fourteen

½ cup egg whites   3 cups dessicated coconut
1¼ cups sugar   7 tsp flour

To prepare the macaroons: Mix the egg whites, the sugar and the coconut in a stainless steel bowl. Set the bowl over simmering water, stirring constantly until the mixture reaches 111 degrees F. Remove the bowl from the heat and stir in the flour. Let the mixture stand for 20 minutes. Preheat oven to 400 degrees F. Using a pastry bag with a #5 or #6 star tube, pipe the mixture onto a well-buttered cookie pan. Bake the macaroons just until golden brown. The cookies should be crunchy on the outside and soft-moist inside.

—Marcel Walter
Colonial Williamsburg
Williamsburg

Currant Cookies

yields about twenty-four

3 TBSP currants   1 egg
4 TBSP rum   1 pinch salt
⅓ cup sugar   ⅔ cup flour
4 TBSP butter

To prepare the cookies: Soak the currants in the rum for thirty minutes. Preheat oven to 350 degrees F. Drain and reserve the rum. In a stainless steel bowl beat the sugar and the butter until the mixture is light and fluffy. Add the egg, the reserved rum, and the salt, beating continuously. Fold in the flour and the currants. With a teaspoon, drop the batter two inches apart onto a buttered cookie sheet. Flatten the mounds with a spoon dipped in cold water. Bake the cookies for 8 to 10 minutes, until the edges are light brown. Remove the cookies from the oven and allow them to cool for 2 minutes on the baking sheet. Transfer the cookies to a rack and cool completely.

—Richard J. Nelson
Richmond

Pecan Bars

yields about eighteen

Sugar dough
1½ cups (3 sticks) butter
    (room temperature)
¾ cup sugar
2 eggs
1 lemon (rind, grated)
1½ cups bread flour
½ tsp baking powder

Step two
1 cup (2 sticks) butter
½ lb. light brown sugar
½ lb. honey

Step three
1 lb. pecan pieces
¼ cup heavy cream

To prepare the sugar dough: Preheat oven to 400 degrees F. Cream the butter with the sugar, the eggs and the grated lemon rind until smooth. Add the flour and the baking powder and chill before using. Line the bottom and sides of a greased 9-by-13-inch baking sheet with the sugar dough. Prick the dough. Bake the sugar dough for approximately 15 minutes, or until half baked.

To prepare step two: In a deep saucepan, combine the cup of butter, the brown sugar and the honey. Boil the mixture for about 3 minutes. Remove the saucepan from the heat.

To prepare the pecan bars: Add the pecan pieces and the heavy cream to step two and, using a wooden spoon or a flexible spatula, spread the mixture evenly over the half-baked sugar dough. Bake for about 35 minutes. Cool and cut into little squares.

—Rolf Herion
Colonial Williamsburg
Williamsburg

DINAH KNEADING DOUGH

I have seen full many a sight
Born of day or drawn by night;
Sunlight on a silver stream,
Golden lilies all a-dream,
Lofty mountains, bold and proud,
Veiled beneath the lacelike cloud;
But no lovely sight I know
Equals Dinah kneading dough.

Brown arms buried elbow-deep
Their domestic rhythm keep,
As with steady sweep they go
Through the gently yielding dough.

Maids may vaunt their finer charms—
Naught to me like Dinah's arms;
Girls may draw, or paint, or sew—
I love Dinah kneading dough.

Eyes of jet and teeth of pearl,
Hair, some say, too tight a-curl;
But the dainty maid I deem
Very near perfection's dream.
Swift the works, and only flings
Me a glance—the least of things.
And I wonder, does she know
That my heart is in the dough?

—Paul Laurence Dunbar
1901

CUSTARDS, FRUIT, & OTHERS

> *strawberries come to table. note this is
> the first year of their bearing having been
> planted in the spring of 1766. and on
> average the plants bear 20. strawberries
> each. 100 fill half a pint.*
>
> —Thomas Jefferson
> May 28, 1767

La Mousse aux Fraises

serves four

1 lb. fresh strawberries	1¼ cups sugar
4 med. egg whites	1 cup heavy cream

To prepare the mousse: Clean, hull, and wash the berries. Run the berries through a food mill to purée and remove the seeds. Whip the egg whites in a bowl with a hand whisk or an egg beater. Slowly add the sugar. Beat until the egg whites are stiff and all of the sugar has been well mixed in. Fold in the strawberry purée. Whip the cream for later use. Spoon the mousse into champagne glasses or dessert dishes and chill. When ready to serve, decorate the mousse with the unsweetened whipped cream.

—Paul Elbling
La Petite France
Richmond

La Tarte Aux Myrtilles

serves four

Crust
1½ cups flour
⅛ tsp salt
¼ cup shortening
5 TBSP butter
½ cup cold water

Filling
1 lb. blueberries
½ cup sugar
1 cup milk
4 eggs
1 tsp vanilla extract

To prepare the crust: Preheat the oven to 400 degrees F. Mix the flour and the salt together in a large bowl. Cut in the shortening and the butter until the mixture is like coarse meal. Add the water and mix until the pastry forms a ball. Let the pastry rest for 15 minutes. Roll the pastry out on a floured board to fit a 9-inch pie pan greased with 1 TBSP butter.

To prepare the tart: Carefully wash and dry the blueberries. Do not pinch or mash the berries. Fill the bottom of the pie crust with blueberries. In a bowl, mix the sugar, the milk, the eggs, and the vanilla. Pour this mixture over the blueberries. Bake the tart for 1 hour.

—Paul Elbling
La Petite France
Richmond

Fresh Lemon Ice Cream

yields one quart

2 cups milk
1 cup sugar, divided
1½ cups heavy cream

1 TBSP lemon zest
6 egg yolks
1 cup fresh lemon juice

To prepare the ice cream: In a saucepan, combine the milk, ½ cup of the sugar, the heavy cream and the zest. On medium heat, bring the mixture just to a boil. Meanwhile, in a stanless steel bowl, beat the yolks and the remaining ½ cup of sugar until thick and lemon-colored. Temper the hot mixture into the cold. Return the mixture to the saucepan and heat to 185 degrees F. Cool the mixture immediately. When the mixture is cool, stir in the lemon juice and freeze in an ice cream freezer.

—Andrew O'Connell
The Trellis
WIlliamsburg

White Chocolate Ice Cream

yields two quarts

½ lb. white chocolate (chopped)
1 cup milk
2 cups heavy cream

1 cup half and half
8 egg yolks
½ cup sugar

To prepare the ice cream: In a double boiler, melt the white chocolate with the milk. Remove from the heat and stir well. In a saucepan, heat the half and half and the heavy cream to a low boil. Meanwhile, in a stainless steel bowl, beat the egg yolks with the sugar until thick and lemon-colored. Stir the cream mixture into the egg yolk mixture, return to the heat, and heat to 185 degrees F. Place the mixture in a stainless steel bowl, stir in the white chocolate mixture, and cool. When cool, freeze the mixture in an ice cream freezer for about 45 minutes.

—Andrew O'Connell
The Trellis
Williamsburg

Rum Cream Custard

serves eight to twelve

2 cups milk
½ cup heavy cream
8 egg yolks
¾ cup sugar

1 pinch salt
1½ tsp vanilla extract
½ cup good white rum

To prepare the custard: Heat the milk and the cream to the scalding point. Beat the egg yolks with the sugar, the salt and the vanilla until well mixed. Add the milk to the egg mixture. In a saucepan or double boiler, cook the mixture, stirring constantly, on low heat until the custard thickens. *Do not boil!* Remove the custard from the heat. Stir in the rum. Serve the custard warm on old-fashioned baked apples filled with raisins and cinnamon.

—Ted Kristensen
The Williamsburg Lodge
Williamsburg

Cranberry Bourbon Sorbet

yields two quarts

3 cups water
2 cups sugar

3 TBSP bourbon
1 lb. whole cranberries

To prepare the sorbet: In a saucepan, bring the water, the sugar and the bourbon to a boil. Allow the mixture to simmer for 5 minutes. Add the cranberries and simmer until the berries pop open. Remove the mixture from the heat and allow to cool. Purée the mixture and press through a fine sieve. Cool the mixture thoroughly and then freeze.

—Marcel Desaulniers
The Trellis
Williamsburg

Daiquiri Sorbet

yields one quart

4 juice oranges
1 grapefruit
½ lemon
1 lime

2 TBSP sugar
1 TBSP coffee cream
1 egg white
2 ounces white rum

To prepare the sorbet: Squeeze the juice from the fruit and remove the seeds. Combine all of the ingredients in a blender and whip on high speed for 20 seconds. Pour the mixture into a stainless steel bowl and put into the freezer. Whisk the mixture every 40 minutes until thick and slushy. Spoon the mixture into a container with a tight-fitting lid and return to the freezer until needed.

—Robert B. Ramsey
Richmond

Lemon Soufflé

serves eight

1½ ounces unflavored gelatin
1 cup cold water
10 egg yolks
1 qt. milk
1 lb. sugar

1 cup lemon juice
1 cup lemon purée
Grated lemon rind from 3 lemons
1 qt. heavy cream (whipped)
Lemon (sliced for garnish)

To prepare the soufflé: Soak the gelatin in cold water. Beat the yolks slightly. In a saucepan or double boiler, combine the milk and the sugar and bring to a boil. Remove the milk mixture from the heat and pour slowly over the egg yolks, stirring constantly and well. Add the soaked gelatin, the lemon juice, purée, and rind. Stir well to dissolve into the mixture and strain. Surround the mixture with crushed ice, stirring from time to time. When the mixture begins to set and thicken, fold in the whipped cream, mixing thoroughly. Pour the mixture into ramekins. Decorate the soufflé with whipped cream rosettes and slices of fresh lemon.

—Rolf Herion
Colonial Williamsburg
Williamsburg

Grapes Palmore

serves six to eight

2 lbs. grapes (white, seedless)
¼ cup honey
3 TBSP brandy

1 cup sour cream
1 cup brown sugar

To prepare the grapes: Wash, pick, and thoroughly dry the grapes. Combine the honey and the brandy. Pour this mixture over the grapes and *marinate overnight.* Put the grapes in a serving dish or individual dishes. Top the grapes with sour cream. Sprinkle with brown sugar and serve chilled.

—Mitford Sims III
The Tobacco Company
Richmond

Sweet Potato Pudding

serves six to eight

2 to 2½ lbs. fresh sweet potatoes
1 egg (beaten thoroughly)
½ cup half and half
⅛ tsp vanilla extract

4 TBSP butter
¼ cup brown sugar
¼ tsp cinnamon
1 dash salt

To prepare the pudding: Wash the sweet potatoes thoroughly. Cut the larger potatoes in half and boil in the jackets until well cooked. Let the potatoes cool, peel them, and mash until quite smooth. Preheat oven to 350 degrees F. Mix the cream and the vanilla with the beaten egg. Set aside. Melt the butter, add the brown sugar, and melt the sugar also. Add the cinnamon and the salt. Set this mixture aside. Combine the egg mixture with the sweet potatoes and mix thoroughly. Add the butter mixture and mix well. Put the mixture in a buttered casserole and bake for 35 to 40 minutes.

—Manfred E. Roehr
Chowning's Tavern
Williamsburg

Southern Delight

serves eight to ten

½ cup (1 stick) sweet butter
  (room temperature)
1 cup confectioner's sugar
1 tsp almond extract
3 egg yolks
24 dark chocolate cookies (crushed)
  as needed

1 pint heavy cream
1 TBSP sugar
3 TBSP dark rum
1 cup pecans (lightly roasted,
  chopped)
3 TBSP miniature chocolate chips

To prepare the delight: Cream the butter, the sugar, and the almond extract. Add the yolks and mix until smooth and fluffy. Line a 7-by-7-by-2-inch serving dish bottom with half of the cookie crumbs and cover them with the butter mixture. Set the dish in the refrigerator. Beat the heavy cream and the sugar until stiff. Fold in the rum, the pecans, and the chocolate chips. Spread the cream mixture on top of the butter mixture. Cover all with the remaining cookie crumbs and *refrigerate overnight.* Serve chilled.

—Marcel Walter
Colonial Williamsburg
Williamsburg

Shenandoah Valley Trifle

serves eight

2 TBSP cornstarch
2 cups plus 1 TBSP sugar
2 cups milk
6 egg yolks
1 tsp vanilla extract
2 TBSP butter

4 cups water
1 stick cinnamon
4 "eating" apples
6 TBSP apricot marmalade
5 TBSP apple brandy
16 ladyfingers

To prepare the custard: Mix the cornstarch with ½ cup plus one TBSP of the sugar. Place the sugar mixture in the top half of a double boiler. Stir in half of the milk and the egg yolks. Then stir in the rest of the milk. Bring the mixture to a boil, stirring at all times. Remove the custard from the heat and mix in the vanilla and the butter. Set the custard aside to cool, stirring frequently.

To prepare the apples: In a saucepan, combine the remaining 1½ cups of sugar with the water and the stick of cinnamon. While the syrup is approaching a boil, pare, halve, and core the apples. Immediately drop the apples in water, acidulated with the juice of one lemon per quart, to prevent discoloration. When the apples are all peeled, remove them from the lemon water and drop into the boiling syrup. Boil the apples for 3 to 6 minutes, until tender. Carefully remove the apples and drain on paper towels, reserving 5 TBSP of the syrup. Combine the syrup with the apple brandy.

To prepare the trifle: Spread three TBSP of the apricot marmalade on the bottom of a 2½-quart serving dish. Place the ladyfingers on top of the layer of marmalade so that they are touching each other, filling in the spaces with cut ladyfingers. Moisten the ladyfingers with the brandy and syrup mixture. Spread the remaining marmalade. Arrange the apples on top of the marmalade. Cover the trifle with the custard and decorate with whipped cream and walnuts.

—Marcel Walter
Colonial Williamsburg
Williamsburg

Holiday Pumpkin Nut Bread with Orange Glace

yields one 9 x 9 x 4 loaf

7 TBSP vegetable shortening
1 cup sugar
1 cup plus 1 TBSP pumpkin purée
1 cup plus 1 TBSP cake flour
2 tsp baking powder
2 tsp cinnamon
1 tsp ground ginger
½ tsp nutmeg
½ tsp salt

¼ cup buttermilk
½ cup whole eggs
½ cup pecans or walnuts (chopped)
½ cup raisins

Orange glace
1 cup confectioner's sugar
2 tsp orange peel (grated)
2 to 3 TBSP orange juice

To prepare the bread: Preheat oven to 325 degrees F. Place the shortening, the sugar, and the pumpkin purée in a mixing bowl. Mix with a paddle

129

on medium speed for 5 minutes. Measure the flour, the baking powder, the cinnamon, the ginger, and the salt and sift these dry ingredients together. Add the dry ingredients to the batter and incorporate. Add the buttermilk and the eggs and mix on the same speed for an additional 5 minutes. Mix in the nuts and the raisins. Pour the batter into a buttered or paper-lined 9-by-9-by-4-inch loaf pan. Bake the loaf for 1 hour or until a knife inserted into the loaf comes out clean.

To prepare the glace: Mix the sugar, the orange peel, and the juice well. Spread the glace over the warm loaves.

—Marcel Walter
Colonial Williamsburg
Williamsburg

SAUCES

Sauce Suprême (White Sauce)

yields one quart

1 cup (2 sticks) butter
½ cup flour
1 qt. milk (hot)

To prepare the sauce: In a saucepan, melt the butter. Add the flour, blending well. Slowly add the hot milk and simmer well, stirring occasionally.

—Ted Kristensen
The Williamsburg Lodge
Williamsburg

Sauce Mornay

yields one quart

3 TBSP butter
3 TBSP flour
1 tsp salt
1 tsp ground white pepper

4 cups milk
3 egg yolks
½ lb. Gruyere *or* Parmesan cheese

To make the sauce: In a saucepan melt the butter; add the flour, the salt, and the pepper. Stir well. Gradually add the milk, stirring constantly until the sauce boils. Set aside. Beat the egg yolks one by one into the mixture and then fold the grated cheese carefully into the sauce with a rubber spatula. It is important to use the spatula, as the cheese will become stringy if it is beaten into the sauce with a whisk. Fold the cheese in very gently.

—Paul Elbling
La Petite France
Richmond

Hollandaise Sauce

yields two and one-half cups

4 egg yolks
1 TBSP cold water
2 cups (4 sticks) butter,
  clarified (warmed)

Juice of one lemon
Salt and cayenne pepper
  to taste

To make the sauce: In a stainless steel bowl, whip the egg yolks and the water together. Place the bowl over a pan of boiling water or in a double boiler, making sure the bottom of the bowl does not touch the water. Whip the egg yolks until cooked to a soft peak. Stir the egg yolks down from the edges and up from the bottom of the bowl. Remove the bowl from the heat. Slowly pour the butter into the eggs, whipping to blend. Add the lemon juice, the cayenne pepper, and the salt, as needed, to taste.

—Richard J. Nelson
Richmond

Stock—Fond de Base Pour Sauce

yields one quart

1 onion
1 garlic clove
1 stalk celery
1 carrot
1 leek (optional)
1 small branch parsley
1 gallon water

2 bay leaves
1 lb. chicken or veal bones (see note)
1 tsp thyme
1 tsp white pepper
1 tsp salt
1 clove

To prepare the stock: Quarter the onion, crush the garlic, and cut the celery stalk and the carrot into 1-inch pieces. Place all of the ingredients in a large stock pot. Bring to a boil and allow to simmer for 1 hour. Strain the liquid. To concentrate, return the strained stock to the heat and reduce to desired strength. Refrigerate until needed.

—Paul Elbling
La Petite France
Richmond

Note: Substitute beef bones for beef stock, fish bones for fish stock.

Crème Fraiche

yields three TBSP

1½ TBSP sour cream
1½ TBSP heavy cream

To make the sauce: Combine the sour cream with the cream. Let the mixture stand at a warm room temperature for 12 hours. Refrigerate until needed.

—Marcel Desaulniers
The Trellis
Williamsburg

Sauce Brune (Brown Sauce)

yields one quart

1 onion
1 garlic clove
1 stalk celery
1 lb. bones (beef, veal, *or* chicken *or* a mixture of the three)
2 bay leaves
1 tsp thyme

½ tsp marjoram leaves
2 fresh tomatoes
2 TBSP flour
2 cups Burgundy wine
1 TBSP tomato purée, *or*
1½ tsp tomato paste
½ gal. water

To prepare the sauce: Preheat the oven to 450 degrees F. Quarter the onion, crush the garlic clove, cut the celery stalk into 1-inch sections, and chop the tomatoes coarsely. Place the bones, the onion, the garlic, the celery, the bay leaves, the thyme, the marjoram, and the tomatoes into a pot roast pan and bake, uncovered, until lightly browned. Sprinkle the flour over the mixture and bake for 10 to 15 minutes. Place the pot roast pan on top of the stove. Add the wine, the purée, and the water. Bring the mixture to a boil and simmer, uncovered, for two hours. Strain. This sauce is an excellent base for any kind of meat sauce. The sauce will keep for up to 4 weeks in the refrigerator and freezes well.

—Paul Elbling
La Petite France
Richmond

BEVERAGES

> *Wine*
>
> *There are two kinds of grapes that the soile doth yeeld naturally: the one is small and sowre of the ordinarie bignesse as ours in England: the other farre greater & of himselfe lushious sweet. When they are plated and husbandeg as they ought, a principall commoditie of wines by them may be raised.*
>
> —Thomas Hariot
> *A briefe and true report of the newfound land of Virginia,* 1588

Brandied Peach Punch

serves four

1 cup brandy	1 tsp sugar
2 ounces peach brandy	1 banana
2 ounces fresh lemon juice	1½ cups club soda

To make the punch: Combine all of the ingredients in a blender and blend on high speed for 10 seconds. Pour over ice cubes and garnish with a fresh peach slice.

—Robert B. Ramsey
Richmond

Raspberry and Strawberry Wine

yields two quarts

2 pints fresh ripe red raspberries
2 pints fresh ripe strawberries
   (stems removed)
1½ lbs. sugar, divided

2 qts. boiling water
1½ TBSP yeast
1 cup fine brandy or cognac

To make the wine: Put the fruit in a ceramic crock or enamel pot. Pour ¾ of a pound of sugar over the fruit. As soon as the water comes to a boil, pour it into the crock. Cover the crock with a double thickness of cheesecloth. *After 3 days* strain the fruit, reserving the liquid. Press on the fruit to remove all of the juice, taking care not to squeeze fruit onto the liquid. A small amount of pulp will not hurt the wine. Return the juice to the crock. Stir in the remaining ¾ pound of sugar. Add the yeast. Cover the crock with cheesecloth, binding the top tightly with string. Keep the crock in a warm place (70 to 75 degrees F.). *After 3 weeks,* or when the liquid stops bubbling, add the brandy. *After 24 hours,* strain the liquid through a siphon hose into mason jars, being careful to avoid matter at the top and residue at the bottom. Seal the jars tightly and hold for *at least a month.* Serve chilled to good friends.

—Jonathan A. Zearfoss
The Trellis
Williamsburg

Jamaican Party Punch

serves eight

1 qt. fresh squeezed orange juice
1 lime (juiced)
1 lemon (juiced)
1 grapefruit (juiced)

1 TBSP sugar
½ cup tonic water
1½ ounces dark Jamaican rum
½ cup white rum

To make the punch: Combine all of the ingredients and shake vigorously. Pour the punch over crushed ice and garnish with a lime slice.

—Robert B. Ramsey
Richmond

137

Toasted Russian Quaaludes

serves four

4 cups percolated coffee
2 ounces Stolichnaya vodka
3 ounces Bailey's Irish Cream
1 ounce Tia Maria (coffee liqueur)

3 ounces Frangelico (hazelnut
  liqueur)
Whipped cream for garnish
Grated nutmeg for garnish

To make the drink: Combine all the ingredients in a small saucepot and warm together. *Do not boil!* Garnish with whipped cream and dust with grated nutmeg.

—Robert B. Ramsey
Richmond

Hot Summer Night

serves four

8 ounces (1 cup) gold tequila
2 cups fresh grapefruit juice

3 cups crushed ice
2 limes

To prepare the cooler: Cut one lime into eight wedges, reserving one wedge for each drink. Squeeze the juice from one lime. Mix the tequila, the grapefruit juice, the crushed ice, the juice from one lime, and four wedges of the other lime (skin and all) in a blender until smooth. Garnish each with a lime wedge and serve.

—Philip Delaplane
The Trellis
Williamsburg

Sunday Morning Strawberry Elixir

serves eight

⅔ bottle (2 cups) white zinfandel
3 pints fresh strawberries (stems
  removed)
2 ounces Grand Marnier

To prepare the elixir: Purée the strawberries briefly in a food processor or blender. Add the chilled wine and the liqueur. Purée on high speed. Serve cool.

—Marcel Desaulniers
The Trellis
Williamsburg

98th Drink not nor talk with your mouth full neither Gaze about you while you are a Drinking

—George Washington
Rules of Civility, 1745

SIDE DISHES

Virginia Ham and Shiitake Mushroom Biscuits

yields two dozen

1 tsp shallots (minced)
1 cup (2 sticks) butter, divided
½ cup Virginia ham (fine dice)
½ cup shiitake mushrooms
   (fine dice)

3 cups flour
1¼ TBSP baking powder
½ tsp salt
½ tsp baking soda
1 cup buttermilk

To prepare the biscuits: Preheat the oven to 325 degrees F. Heat the shallots in 2 TBSP butter, until transparent. Add the ham and the mushrooms. Sauté for about 3 minutes. Set aside to cool completely. Mix the flour, the baking powder, the salt, and the soda. Cut in the butter until the mixture is mealy. Add the cooled ham and mushroom mixture and mix completely. Make a well in the center and add the buttermilk all at once. Stir only until the ingredients cling together. Roll out the dough to a thickness of ¾ inch and cut into desired shapes. Bake the biscuits on a cookie sheet for 25 to 30 minutes or until done.

—Andrew O'Connell
The Trellis
Williamsburg

Bacon Scallion Cornbread

serves eight

½ lb. bacon (sliced)
1 bunch scallions
1½ cups cornmeal (white or yellow)
¾ cup flour
2 tsp baking powder

1 tsp salt
½ cup sour cream
2 med. eggs
1½ cups buttermilk

To prepare the cornbread: Preheat the oven to 350 degrees F. Cook the bacon for 8 to 10 minutes or until crisp. Drain the fat, reserving one TBSP. Crumble the bacon. This should yield about ½ cup. Clean the scallions by removing the root end and then washing. Slice the scallions on an angle. Combine the cornmeal, the flour, the baking powder, and the scallions. To this mixture add the buttermilk. Put the one TBSP of bacon fat in a 9-inch cast iron skillet and heat the skillet in the oven for 5 minutes. Mix the dry ingredients thoroughly with the wet ingredients. Add the batter to the hot skillet and bake for 20 to 25 minutes or until golden brown and firm. Cut the bread into eight wedges.

—Jeff Duncan
The Trellis
Williamsburg

Grilled Nut Butter and Jelly

serves one

2 slices bread
1 TBSP butter (room temperature)

1½ ounces nut butter
Jelly or fresh fruit as needed

For the nut butter: Store-bought is fine, but fresh ground is best. Try cashews, almonds, or pistachios or a combination. Toast the nuts and then grind or purée in a food processor.

For the jelly: From a jar is all right, but in season, fresh fruit (try strawberries or raspberries) is the best. Clean and slice the fruit before putting in the sandwich.

To prepare the sandwich: Put the nut butter and the fruit in the middle of the two slices of bread. Smear the butter on the outside and grill the sandwich for 2 to 3 minutes on each side.

—Philip Delaplane
The Trellis
Williamsburg

John's Favorite Potatoes

serves four

¼ cup peanut oil, divided
4 garlic cloves (minced)
½ tsp dry mustard
2 tsp thyme (fresh), *or*
   1 tsp oregano (dry)
½ tsp cayenne pepper

1 tsp black pepper (fresh ground)
2 tsp salt
4 potatoes (peeled)
4 shallots (sliced)
4 TBSP unsalted sweet butter

To prepare the potatoes: Preheat the oven to 400 degrees F. Use two TBSP of peanut oil to grease the baking sheet. To the remaining peanut oil, add the garlic, the mustard, the fresh thyme, the cayenne, the black pepper, and the salt. Cut the potatoes in half lengthwise. Slice the potatoes across as thinly as possible and press down to fan out. Lifting the potatoes on the side of the knife, place them on a baking sheet side by side in two rows. Mold the potatoes slightly to allow no room between them. Pour the peanut oil mixture to coat the tops. Place the sliced shallots in the valleys between the potatoes. Cut the butter into small chunks and distribute the chunks on top of the shallots. Bake the potatoes until brown and crispy, approximately 40 to 50 minutes.

—Jonathan A. Zearfoss
The Trellis
Williamsburg

Pommes de Terre Amadines

serves eight

3 lb. sweet potatoes
2 eggs (beaten)

Salt and pepper to taste
Sliced blanched almonds

To prepare the sweet potatoes: Boil the sweet potatoes until they are tender. Peel and mash. Return the sweet potatoes to the stove. Add the eggs, mixing well. Season to taste with salt and pepper. Cook on medium, stirring occasionally until the mixture thickens. Remove the pot from the heat. Preheat oven to 350 degrees F. Shape the sweet potato mixture into small cones. Roll the cones in the sliced almonds and place on a baking pan. Bake the sweet potatoes for 15 minutes.

—Richard Nelson
Richmond

Potatoes with Fruit

serves six

4 TBSP butter or margarine
3 med. potatoes (boiled and sliced)
2 green onions (chopped)
1 mango (sliced)
½ cup coconut (grated)
1 nectarine (sliced)

½ lemon (for juice)
1 TBSP garlic (minced)
Salt and white pepper to taste
6 leaves iceberg lettuce
1 red pepper (sliced)
1 TBSP dill (chopped)

To prepare the potatoes: In a pan, melt the butter or margarine. Add the slices of potato in a step-like arrangement. Add the green onion, the mango slices, the coconut and the nectarine. Sprinkle the mixture with the lemon juice and the garlic. Season with salt and pepper. Cook the potatoes, covered, on low, for 15 to 20 minutes. Remove the pan from the heat. On six individual plates, place a bed of iceberg. Distribute the mixture evenly amongst the lettuce leaves. Sprinkle each plate with dill. Place one slice of red pepper on top.

—Gideon Hirteinstein
Guest Services, Inc.
Washington, D.C.

Brown Rice Pilaf

yields 4½ cups

1½ cups raw brown rice
3 cups chicken stock
1 tsp tumeric
¼ cup currants

¼ cup Madeira
½ cup scallions (minced)
⅓ cup pinenuts (toasted)
1 TBSP minced preserved ginger

To prepare the rice: Put the rice and the chicken stock in a medium saucepan. Bring the stock to a boil and then simmer the mixture for 45 minutes. Remove the saucepan from the heat and allow to stand for 10 minutes. Soak the currants in the Madeira for 30 minutes. Drain, and combine the currants with the rice. Stir in the scallions, the pinenuts, and the ginger. Serve.

—Mitford Sims III
The Tobacco Company
Richmond

Herb Rice

serves four to six

1½ TBSP butter
1 small onion (fine dice)
1 TBSP basil (fresh chopped)
1 TBSP parsley (fresh chopped)

1 TBSP tarragon (fresh chopped)
2 cups white rice
4 cups chicken stock *or* water

To prepare the rice: In a saucepan, melt the butter. Add the onion and the herbs and sauté for 1 minute. Add the rice and stir to coat the rice with butter. Add the stock and bring to a boil. Reduce the heat, cover, and cook for 20 minutes.

—George Francisco, apprentice
The Trellis
Williamsburg

Peppered Black-Eyed Peas

serves four to six

1 lb. black-eyed peas
2 strips bacon (small dice)
4 cups chicken stock
1 green pepper (small dice)
1 red pepper (small dice)
1 jalapeño pepper

1 med. onion (small dice)
1 small leek (white part, diced)
½ tsp cayenne pepper
3 tsp Worcestershire sauce
Salt to taste

To prepare the peas: Twenty-four hours in advance, soak the peas in enough water to cover plus two cups. Fry the bacon to render fat in a heavy half gallon pot. Add the peas and the chicken stock. Bring the stock to a boil and then add the peppers, the onion, the leek, the cayenne pepper, and the Worcestershire sauce. Cook the peas for about 30 minutes or until done to taste.

—George Francisco, apprentice
The Trellis
Williamsburg

Wild Rice Pancakes

serves six

1 cup salted water
⅓ cup wild rice, (rinsed thoroughly)
2 cups milk
2 TBSP butter (melted)
1 tsp salt
4 eggs (separated,
   room temperature)

1 cup (5 ounces) blanched almonds
   (toasted, finely chopped)
1 cup flour
Pinch cream of tartar
2 TBSP (or more) clarified butter *or*
   1 TBSP butter and 1 TBSP
   vegetable oil

To prepare the rice: In a saucepan, bring one cup of salted water to a boil. Add the wild rice, cover, and simmer until the rice is tender and all the water is absorbed, about 45 minutes. The rice can be cooked ahead of time and set aside.

To prepare the pancakes: Blend the milk, the melted butter, and the salt into the rice. Beat the yolks until light in color, about 3 minutes. Mix the yolks into the rice mixture. Stir in the chopped nuts and the flour. Beat the egg whites and the cream of tartar until stiff, but not dry, and fold into the batter. Preheat the oven to 175 degrees F. Heat the two TBSP of clarified butter on a griddle or in a large heavy skillet on medium. Ladle 2½-inch diameter pancakes onto the griddle and cook until the bottom is golden brown and the pancakes begin to set, about 2 to 3 minutes. Turn the pancakes and brown the second side. Repeat with the remaining batter, adding more butter to the griddle as necessary. Arrange the finished pancakes in a single layer on a baking sheet and keep warm in the oven until all the pancakes are cooked. Serve immediately.

—Richard J. Nelson
Richmond

Sweet and Sour Red Cabbage with Apples

serves six

1 head red cabbage (two pounds)
1 smoked ham hock
2 med. apples
2 bay leaves
½ cup red wine vinegar
⅛ tsp pepper
1 TBSP jelly (currant *or* grape)

½ cup brown sugar
¾ tsp allspice
5 whole cloves
1 tsp salt
1 cup red wine
½ cup water

To prepare the cabbage: Rinse the cabbage and remove all of the wilted leaves. Cut the head of cabbage into quarters and remove the core. Shred the cabbage coarsely and place it into a large pot. Add the ham hock. Core and dice the apples (do not remove the skin) and add to the pot. Add the bay leaves, the vinegar, the pepper, the jelly, the sugar, the allspice, the cloves, the salt, the red wine and the water. Cover the pot and bring to a boil. Reduce to a simmer and cook for about 1 hour. For crisper cabbage, remove from the heat earlier. Remove the ham hock and let the cabbage sit to marinate thoroughly. Reheat the cabbage just before serving. The cabbage will taste better when cooked one to two days before serving. The cabbage goes well with many German-style dishes.

—Manfred E. Roehr
Chowning's Tavern
Williamsburg

Sauerkraut with Apples and Caraway Seed

serves six

1 27-ounce can sauerkraut	½ tsp salt
1½ cups white wine	⅛ tsp pepper
1 cup water	2 apples (shredded)
1 tsp caraway seed	1 med. potato (peeled, shredded)
2 tsp brown sugar	1 6-ounce smoked sausage (sliced)

To prepare the sauerkraut: Drain the sauerkraut and wash thoroughly with cold water. Combine the wine, the water, the caraway seed, the brown sugar, the salt and the pepper. Bring the mixture to a boil. Add the drained sauerkraut to the boiling mixture. Add the apple. Reduce to simmer. Add the potato and the sliced smoked sausage. Let the mixture simmer for about 2 hours, or until very tender. Drain and serve. The shredded potato will provide a shining or glazed appearance to the sauerkraut.

—Manfred E. Roehr
Chowning's Tavern
Williamsburg

Tomato and Basil Pasta

yields one pound

¾ cup tomato paste
2 TBSP basil (fresh chopped)
1 TBSP olive oil

2½ cups flour
½ tsp salt
2 large eggs

To prepare the pasta: Place the tomato paste, the basil, and the olive oil in a mixing bowl. Add the flour and the salt. With a dough hook or by hand, knead for 1 minute. Add the eggs one at a time and continue to knead until the dough forms a ball. Remove the dough from the bowl and knead by hand until soft, dusting the kneading surface lightly with flour as necessary. Cover the dough and allow to relax for 1 hour under refrigeration. Roll and cut the pasta into desired pasta shape. The cut pasta, tossed with cornmeal, may be held under refrigeration for two days. Before cooking, gently toss the pasta to remove excess cornmeal.

—Marcel Desaulniers
The Trellis
Williamsburg

Fresh Pumpkin Pasta

yields one pound

6 ounces pumpkin (peeled, raw)
2⅓ cups flour
½ tsp salt

1 TBSP olive oil
2 large eggs

To prepare the pasta: Cook the pumpkin in boiling, salted water until soft, approximately 15 minutes. Purée the pumpkin in a blender or food processor. Allow the pumpkin to cool. In a mixing bowl combine the pumpkin, the flour, the salt, and the olive oil and knead by hand or with a dough hook for one minute. Add the eggs one at a time and knead until the dough forms a ball. Remove the dough from the mixing bowl and knead by hand until soft, dusting the kneading surface lightly with flour as necessary. Cover the dough and allow it to relax for 1 hour under refrigeration. Roll and cut the dough into the desired pasta shape. The cut pasta, tossed with cornmeal, may be held under refrigeration for two days. Before cooking, gently toss the pasta to remove excess cornmeal.

—Marcel Desaulniers
The Trellis
Williamsburg

Gouda Polenta

yields one dozen

4 ounces (¼ lb.) Gouda cheese
½ cup (1 stick) salted butter
4 cups (1 qt.) milk
1 cup fine white cornmeal

½ tsp nutmeg
1 tsp black pepper, (coarse ground)
½ cup heavy cream
1 tsp salt

To prepare the polenta: Chop half of the cheese. Divide the remainder into twelve slices and set aside. Lightly butter twelve ⅓-cup muffin molds. Set aside. In a saucepan, melt the butter. Mix in the milk. Bring to a slow boil stirring constantly until the mixture coats a wooden spoon. Add the cornmeal quickly, using a wire whisk to mix the meal with milk. Continue cooking over medium heat, stirring with a wooden spoon until the mixture is the consistency of a very thick porridge. Beat in the nutmeg, the pepper, and the chopped cheese. Continue beating until all lumps are dissolved and the mixture is smooth. Remove the polenta from the heat and beat in the cream and the salt. Spoon the mixture into the buttered molds. Tap the molds gently against the counter to settle the mixtures and relase the air bubbles. Allow to sit for 15 minutes to allow the molds to shape. Preheat the oven to 400 degrees F. Lightly butter a heavy ovenproof skillet and turn the molds into it. Place a slice of cheese on top of each mold. Heat over low heat for a few minutes to melt the cheese (the cheese should soak into the mold, however, do not allow it to run down the sides). Place the skillet in the pre-heated oven for about 15 minutes (until the molds begin to swell). Glaze the cheese tops under the broiler and serve immediately.

—Mark W. Kimmel
The Tobacco Company
Richmond

. . . Some tawny Ceres, goddess of her days, (maize,
First learned with stones to crack the well-dry'd
Thro' the sieve to shake the golden show'r,
In boiling water stir the yellow flour.
The yellow flour, bestrew'd and stir'd with haste,
Swell in the flood and thickens to a paste,
Then puffs and wallops, rises to the brim,
Drinks the dry knobs that on the surface swim:
The knobs at last the busy ladle breaks,
And the whole mass its true consistence takes.

. . . Let the green Succatash with thee contend,
Let beans and corn their sweetest juices blend,
Let butter drench them in its yellow tide,
And a long slice of bacon grace their side;
Not all the plate, how fam'd soe'er it be,
Can please my palate like a bowl of thee.
Some talk of Hoe-cake, fair Virginia's pride,
Rich Johnny-cake this mouth has often tri'd;

. . . The yellow bread, whose face like amber glows,
And all of Indian that the bake-pan knows—
You tempt me not—my fav'rite greets my eyes,
To that lov'd bowl my spoon by instinct flies.

—Joel Barlow
"Hasting Pudding," 1793

ABOUT THE CHEFS

Otto Bernet—A Certified Master Pastry Chef since 1983 and member of the American Academy of Chefs, Otto runs Chef Otto's Bakery for the Tobacco Company in Richmond. Otto, who is the Chairman of the Board of the Virginia Chef's Association, is a former Chef of the Year (1980) and a past President (1983–84) as well as Vice-President (1981–82) and Treasurer for five years. In addition to participating in numerous international shows, Otto has been on television demonstrations several times. Otto previously ran the La Petite France Pastry Shop for Chef Paul Elbling. Born in Switzerland, Otto has been a citizen of the United States since 1964.

Swiss Onion Pie (Zwiebelkuchen), page 24
Swiss Meat Pie, page 89
Fondue, page 97–98
Chilled Strawberry Meringue Cake
 (Sacherin aux Fraises), page 113

George W. Clarke III—Assistant Chef at the Country Club of Virginia, in Richmond, where he has been employed since 1971, George has received culinary training in the United States Coast Guard, the Richmond Technical Center, and the Culinary Institute of America. George's goal is to be a Certified Master Chef.

Chicken with Sausage and Almonds, page 81

Arthur C. Cook III—Treasurer of the Virginia Chef's Association and Chairman of the Culinary Arts Committee. Art is the Chef at Richmond's Westwood Racquet Club. Art served in the United States Marine Corps before studying Food Science at Tuskeegee Institute. Art has been Chef at a number of restaurants in the Richmond area.

Spiced Meatball and Bean Soup, page 5
Fish Chowder, page 12
Baked Onions with Meat Stuffing, page 25
Stuffed Deviled Clams, page 24
Zucchini Salad, page 43–44
Rabbit Fricassee, page 79
Chicken à la Art Suprême, page 79–80
Duckling with Sausage Stuffing, page 77–78

Philip K. Delaplane—Phil, whose motto is "Work harder, work faster, do more," is Chef at the Trellis Restaurant in Williamsburg where he has been employed since 1981. Before Phil was hired as Assistant Chef at the Trellis, he had previously owned and run the Sunshine Deli in Manitou Springs, Colorado as well as cooking at a number of establishments including the Keystone resort in Keystone, Colorado and the Williamsburg Inn.

Marcel Desaulniers—Executive Chef and co-owner of the Trellis Restaurant in Williamsburg, Marcel is the current President of the Virginia Chef's Association and the 1986 Chef of the Year. Marcel graduated from the Culinary Institute of America in 1965, before serving in Vietnam in the United States Marine Corps. Marcel was manager of Food Production and Quality Control for Colonial Williamsburg (1972-74) and has been named to *Food and Wine* magazine's Honor Roll of American Chefs (1983) and *Cooks Magazine*'s "Who's Who of Cooking in America" (1984). Marcel travels often and has spoken at Symposiums on American Cuisine in New Orleans and San Francisco as well as at the October 1985 Commencement at the Culinary Institute of America.

Jeff Duncan—An apprentice at Colonial Williamsburg from 1975 until 1977, Jeff was employed at Chez Pierre in Virginia Beach after his graduation. Jeff worked at the Keystone resort in Colorado (1978–81). Since 1981, Jeff has worked at the Trellis in Williamsburg where he was appointed an Assistant Chef in the autumn of 1982. Planning to be certified, Jeff would eventually like to open a restaurant of his own. It is his belief that success in that venture depends on "making the food you serve—The Best."

Rabbit and White Bean Soup, page 8
Jeff's Potato Salad, page 49
Bacon and Scallion Cornbread, page 143

Paul Elbling—A Master Chef and a recognized wine expert, Paul began his career as an apprentice in Strasbourg, France. Chef Paul has traveled extensively and was instrumental in the development of the apprentice program in Virginia. He is a past President of the Virginia Chef's Association as well as Chef of the Year (1977). Chef Paul Elbing owns and operates La Petite France in Richmond. Chef Paul has noted the similarity of the Virginia countryside to that of his native Alsace. In his own cookbook, Paul reminds us to "Relax, bring gusto, warmth, and good humor, into your kitchen with a smile..."

Rolf Herion—A native of the Black Forest, affable Rolf is Executive Pastry Chef and Manager of the Bakery for Colonial Williamsburg, where he has been employed for over twenty-four years. Rolf believes in treating every Colonial Williamsburg visitor, and not just the kings and queens, like a dignitary. Rolf was the Virginia Chef's Association Chef of the Year (1978).

Gideon Hirteinstein—A Certified Executive Chef, Gideon graduated with distinction from Culinary School in 1969. Gideon did his apprenticeship in a five-star hotel in Israel. He has been Chef in a number of restaurant and resort operations, including the Zim Lines Israelean Company. Gideon came to the United States in 1982 and is presently taking his second cookbook to press. Gideon is currently employed as Executive Chef by Guests Services, Inc. in the D.C. area.

Mark W. Kimmel—A 1974 graduate of the Culinary Institute of America, Mark is the Executive Chef at the Tobacco Company in Richmond. Currently the Virginia Chef's Association Apprenticeship Committee Chairman, Mark was Chef of the Year (1981) as well as Certification Chairman from 1980 to 1984. Before working at the Tobacco Company, Mark was Executive Chef for the Fripp Island Company in Fripp Island, South Carolina.

> *Seafood Gumbo, page 12*
> *Seafood Quiche, page 19*
> *Mushrooms Nantua, page 27*
> *Tropicale Salad with Curried Chutney Dressing, page 45–46*
> *Tobacco Company House Dressing, page 40*
> *Crabmeat Raphael, page 66*
> *Crab Vanderbilt with Mornay Sauce, page 65*
> *Indonesian Shrimp Sauté, page 67–68*
> *Chili, page 90*
> *Gouda Polenta, page 150*

Ted Kristensen—Originally from Jutland, Denmark, Ted received his culinary training at the Grand Hotel in Stockholm, Sweden. Ted has held numerous positions as Chef in the hotel and travel industry, and is currently Executive Chef of the Williamsburg Lodge. Ted was the Virginia Chef's Association Chef of the Year in 1983 and a member of the Resort Food Executive Committee for four years.

> *Gazpacho, page 14–15*
> *Seafood Chowder, page 11*
> *Chilled Strawberry Soup, page 16*
> *Cherry Soup, page 15*
> *Chicken Livers in Red Wine Wrapped in Bacon, page 18*
> *Seafood Salad Dressing, page 41*
> *Chicken Salad Imperial, page 45*
> *Flounder Walewska, page 61*
> *Rum Cream Custard, page 124*
> *White Sauce (Sauce Suprême), page 132*

Rhys H. Lewis—Rhys, who graduated from the Culinary Institute of America in 1977, is currently a Sous Chef at the Williamsburg Inn. In addition to being Chef Instructor at Holyoke Community College in Holyoke, Massachusetts, Rhys has been employed at the Inn at Huntington in Huntington, Massachusetts, the Frankfurt Intercontinental Hotel in Frankfurt, West Germany, and the Woodstock Inn and Resort in Woodstock, Vermont. Rhys is presently working towards certification.

> *Frühling (Spring) Salad, page 48*
> *Broiled Grouper with Tomatoes, Mushrooms*
>   *and Scallions, page 72–73*
> *Poached Fillet of Salmon with Cucumber*
>   *Julienne and Caviar, page 72*
> *Escallopini of Veal with Lemon and Parmesan, page 96*

Richard J. Nelson—A Certified Executive Chef, Richard is an Honor graduate of the Culinary Institute of America. Virginia Chef's Association Chef of the Year in 1984, Richard won two medals at the 1982 Virginia Culinary Arts Competition.

> *Cream of Squash and Leek Soup, page 5*
> *Artichoke and Broccoli Mousseline with*
>   *Hollandaise Sauce, page 28*
> *Endive Belge Vinaigrette Mimosa, page 44*
> *Scallops Lafayette, page 61–62*
> *Chicken Tarragon, page 83*
> *Currant Cookies, page 118*
> *Wild Rice Pancakes, page 147*
> *Pommes de Terre Amadines, page 144*
> *Hollandaise Sauce, page 133*

163

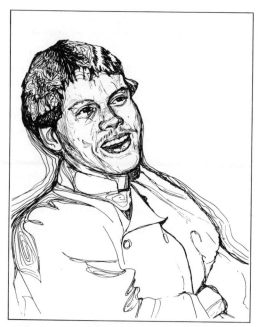

Andrew O'Connell—Employed by the Trellis Restaurant in Williamsburg since 1980, Andrew is presently the Pastry Chef.

164

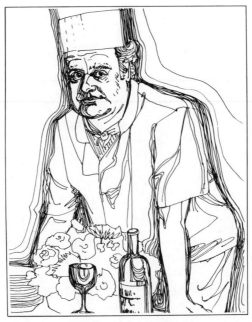

William Pearce—After attending Chef's School in Washington, D.C., Bill apprenticed in the Washington area, cooking at several embassies and catering for government parties. The proprietor of Pearce's Parties, Virginia's only "five star" caterer, this charter member of the Virginia Chef's Association won second prize for the recipe included here in the Virginia State Crab Cake Cook-off. The goal of Pearce's Parties: "...to continue the American spirit and improve and continue to feature American food and recipes."

Stuffed Softshell Crabs Suprême with
Gloucester Sauce, page 64–65

Manfred E. Roehr—Chef of the Year in 1982, Manfred has been President, Vice-President, Sergeant at Arms, and Secretary of the Virginia Chef's Association. Born in Neukirch, Germany, Manfred was cook, Mess Steward, and Mess Sergeant in the United States Army from 1963 to 1970. Presently, Manfred is the Chef and Assistant Manager of Chowning's Tavern in Williamsburg. Manfred received an A.A.S. degree in Hotel Restaurant Institutional Management from Thomas Nelson Community College and became a Certified Executive Chef in 1980. Manfred serves as a judge at Fort Lee Culinary Art Shows.

Hans Schadler—Originally from Hanau am Main, West Germany, the Executive Chef of the Williamsburg Inn is the Virginia Chef's Association Certification Chairman. Formerly an Executive Chef for Rock-resorts, Inc., Hans is a member of the American Academy of Chefs, and is currently President-Secretary of the Resort Hotel Executive Committee. The Central Vermont Chef's Association Chef of the Year in 1980, Hans has received awards in numerous food competitions.

Mitford Sims III—Assistant Chef at the Tobacco Company, Mitford is currently the Vice-President of the Virginia Chef's Association and was Chef of the Year in 1985. The Richmond area New Membership Chairman is active as an instructor in the American Culinary Federation apprenticeship program.

Sauerkraut Balls, page 19–20
Cheese Cookies, page 20
Chocolate Pound Cake, page 104
Black Bottom Cupcakes, page 104
Whole Wheat Pound Cake, page 114
Grapes Palmore, page 126
Brown Rice Pilaf, page 145

Marcel Walter—A Certified Executive Pastry Chef and member of the American Academy of Chefs, this dual citizen of Switzerland and the United States is Pastry Chef for Colonial Williamsburg. Marcel has worked as Pastry Chef in a number of excellent hotels. He has been awarded a number of prizes for his pieces in international competitions, including an award from the city of New Orleans for his participation in 1972 in the preparation of the world's largest ice cream sundae.

Chocolate Pot de Crème "Mary," page 102
Coconut Macaroons, page 118
Shenandoah Valley Trifle, page 128
Southern Delight, page 127
Holiday Pumpkin Nut Bread with Orange Glace,
*   page 129–130*

Paul W. Smith—A Certified Pastry Chef, Paul graduated in 1976 from Cape Cod Community College with an Associate degree in Hotel and Restaurant Management. Currently Assistant Head Pastry Chef at Colonial Wiliamsburg under Rolf Herion, Paul has won numerous prizes for his cakes and pastries.

Caramel-Pecan Cheesecake, page 116

Dominador Valeros—Originally from the Philippines, the Chef of the Virginia Beach Yacht Club has studied at the United States Navy Baking School, the Navy Mess Management School, Tidewater Community College, and The Culinary Institute of America.

Hot Curried Fruit Salad, page 46
Crab Norfolk, page 64
Pork Chops Filipinaña, page 92
Medallions of Beef with Shiitake Mushrooms
*   and Red Wine Sauce, page 88*
Veal, page 94
Pecan Whiskey Cake, page 112
Cake "Sans Rival," page 111

Jonathan A. Zearfoss—Graduated with a B.A. in English from the College of William and Mary in 1982, Jonathan has been employed by the Trellis Restaurant in Williamsburg since its opening in 1980. He was appointed Assistant Chef in the summer of 1984.

INDEX

174